ESSENTIAL
EMPLOYMENT
DOCUMENTS

**Your personal library of
employment contracts,
policies, procedures and letters.**

Indicator
Advisors & Publishers

Calgarth House • 39-41 Bank Street
Ashford • Kent
Tel.: 01233 653500 • Fax: 01233 647100
customer.services@indicator.co.uk • www.indicator.co.uk

ISBN 0-9548140-1-0

Second Edition - E2P3

Introduction

Ever since we started publishing Tips & Advice Personnel back in 1999, we've been literally inundated with requests for sample employment documents. It seems that in this highly regulated and litigious time, every sensible employer wants to make sure he has the right paperwork in place. And if this includes you, then of course you're quite correct. Using the right workplace documents is absolutely vital - not only to ensure that staff are clear about what's what, but also to help keep tribunal applications at bay. One thing we've learned is that employment tribunals are almost fanatical about seeing that the right procedures have been followed and the correct paperwork employed.

So you can see why we decided to produce this book, Essential Employment Documents. In it you'll find more than 100 all-new documents, policies, procedures etc. that you can readily apply in your workplace. Everything from a Recruitment Authorisation Form to a Dismissal Letter is included. As always, they're written in easy to understand language and accompanied by a helpful commentary on when and how they should be used.

In this second edition we've fully updated all our employment documents (plus added several new ones) so that they're fully compliant with the new rules on disciplinary and grievance procedures which take effect on October 1, 2004.

We hope that you'll soon regard this book as an essential, everyday practical guide that will help you to make the most of your principal asset - your workforce. If there are documents that you think we should add, please let us know. We'll be happy to include them in subsequent editions.

Duncan Callow
Managing Editor
Indicator Advisors & Publishers

September 2004

Table of contents

SECTION III - COMPANY RULES AND STAFF HANDBOOKS

ESSENTIAL
EMPLOYMENT
DOCUMENTS

SECTION IV - DISCIPLINARY AND GRIEVANCE PROCEDURES

SECTION V - SICKNESS ABSENCE

Section I

Recruitment
and appointment

Recruitment and appointment

Recruitment of new staff is a time-consuming exercise but it's important not to cut corners. You must ensure that the entire process is conducted properly and fairly to attract the right candidates and to stay on the right side of the law.

BUSINESS REQUIREMENTS

The first stage in recruitment is to always check what your business requirements are. Do you really need a new member of staff and, if so, are you proposing to recruit at the right level of seniority? It's common for line managers to make requests for replacement staff without giving any thought to whether work could be re-distributed or work systems better organised. The *Recruitment Authorisation Form* and *Recruitment Policy* (at the end of this section) will help you with this.

JOB DESCRIPTION AND PERSON SPECIFICATION

The next stage is to draw up a job description and a person specification. These will provide the basic information to draft advertisements and assess candidates. A job description sets out the main details of the job, including job title, job duties and responsibilities. The specimen *Job Description* highlights the information you need to include. A *Person Specification* describes the level of qualification, knowledge, skills, experience and competencies required of the successful candidate. Don't overstate these. Naturally, you want the best candidate for the job but setting unrealistically high achievement levels increases the problem of attracting that person and can result in job dissatisfaction if they later find their talents are under-utilised.

APPLICATION FORMS

If you require candidates to fill in an application form rather than send in their CV, only seek personal information relevant to the recruitment decision and only request information about criminal convictions if that information can be justified in terms of the job on offer. Even if justified, spent convictions do not

have to be declared unless the job falls within an "excepted" category. You can use the **Application Form** as a useful precedent.

ADVERTISING

Consider internal candidates first. If you don't, you risk dissatisfaction amongst the workforce and, ultimately, resignations. When drafting a job ad, aim to attract attention and maintain interest. Make it eye-catching and interesting! Ensure it also covers the essentials of the company, the job, person specification, salary/benefits and location. Finally, don't forget to include how the candidate should apply and whether there's a closing date. Legislation sets out rules you have to comply with to avoid unlawful discrimination when advertising a position. Construct ads in a way that encourages equality of opportunity. For example, avoid stereotyped phrases (e.g. "sales person" rather than "salesman"), don't place ads solely in a newspaper read mainly by one sex or race and don't suggest the successful applicant will not have a disability. Once you've drafted a suitable ad, it needs to be published. The national broadsheets or professional journals are best for managerial, professional and technical jobs. Local papers, trade journals and the Job Centre are preferable for recruiting junior office staff and manual workers. Consider using the Internet too.

RECRUITMENT AGENCIES

Recruitment agencies are useful if you want to relieve the pressure of recruitment. They will deal with the preliminary work of advertising, sift suitable candidates and arrange interview dates. However, they do cost! Typically, an agency's fee will be between 15 and 20% of the employee's first year salary, plus VAT. Do compare fees and always check their terms and conditions of business, particularly those regarding repayment of the fee should the employee resign or be dismissed in the first few months of employment.

SIFTING APPLICATIONS

Once applications have been received, you need to sift them to decide whom to invite to interview. Compare the applications with the key criteria in the person specification. Applications can be sorted into three categories:
- unsuitable (to be rejected – use the **Rejection of Unsuccessful Candidate Before Interview Letter**)
- possible (to be invited to interview – use the **Invitation to Attend Interview Letter**)
- marginal (to be held in reserve).

ACKNOWLEDGEMENT

If this process is likely to take some time, send a standard acknowledgement letter to each applicant. The *Acknowledgement of Application Letter* can be used for this. It's advisable for at least two managers (or one manager and a member of the Human Resources department if you have one) to carry out the selection process so it remains objective and unbiased. A shortlist for interview can then be drawn up and interviews arranged. In scheduling interviews, ensure adequate time is set aside. For junior roles, 30 minutes should suffice. For more senior positions, an hour or more will be required. Sufficient time should be allowed between interviews for discussion to take place and notes to be written up. If you intend to carry out checks to verify any of the information a candidate has provided, for example, the candidate's qualifications, explain the verification process to the candidate. Where verification requires obtaining the release of information from a third party, obtain the applicant's signed consent.

INTERVIEWS

Interviews are a part of the selection process for most employers. You should always have at least two interviewers to minimise the risk of a biased decision. Interviews are most effective at predicting future performance and success in a job where they are properly structured and organised and where the interviewers have been properly trained. This will involve them having prepared in advance a list of questions to be asked of all the candidates, using the job description and the person specification. The questions asked should relate to the requirements of the job and the applicant's particular competencies. You should be aware that unlawful discrimination claims can arise at any stage of the recruitment process and it is therefore not only employees who can bring a claim: unsuccessful job applicants can too. It's unlawful to discriminate against a job applicant at any stage of the recruitment process on the grounds of their sex, marital status, disability, race, sexual orientation or religion.

DISCRIMINATION

Discrimination may take place at the interview stage where, for example, questions are asked based on stereotypical assumptions, sexist or racist remarks are made by the interviewer or unnecessary questions, not relevant to the requirements of the job, are asked of the interviewee. If you are to interview a disabled job applicant, interview and other selection arrangements should be made so as to ensure the disabled applicant is accommodated. Employers who take their equal opportunities responsibilities particularly

seriously may wish to conduct equal opportunities monitoring. The *Equal Opportunities Monitoring Form* can be used for this purpose and it should be kept separate from your main application form in order to remove the risk of discrimination occurring during the recruitment process.

SELECTION TESTS

In addition to a structured interview, it's often worthwhile conducting psychological tests. These can provide more valid and reliable evidence of levels of intelligence, personality characteristics, aptitudes and abilities than can be obtained from interview. The tests are usually scored by reference to the average performance of the group. Avoid do-it-yourself tests and everyone responsible for the application of tests should be properly trained.

MAKING JOB OFFERS AND OBTAINING REFERENCES

After the interview and any testing procedures have been completed and a decision taken on the successful candidate, a job offer can be made, either in writing or over the telephone. If an offer is made verbally over the telephone, also confirm it in writing. You can use the *Offer of Appointment Letter* for this. It's common for job offers to be made conditional on the receipt of satisfactory references or on other information/documentation being provided. Usually at least one work-related reference will be required. References can be requested by using the *Reference Request Form*. Obtain the candidate's authorisation before requesting references.

The unsuccessful interviewees will also need to be rejected. Use the *Rejection of Unsuccessful Candidate After Interview Letter*. After rejection letters have been sent out to the unsuccessful interviewees, their personal information and interview notes should be destroyed within a reasonable period of time. The minimum period of time for which you should preserve recruitment records is until a claim of unlawful discrimination by an unsuccessful applicant is time-barred. This period is three months from the act of discrimination. Therefore, six months is a recommended retention period. If you wish to retain the details of unsuccessful applicants on file for future vacancies, write to them advising them of this and give them the opportunity to have their details removed.

RELOCATION EXPENSES

If you are willing to offer relocation assistance to new recruits, then you may find the *Relocation Policy* of assistance here.

RECRUITMENT AUTHORISATION FORM

Line manager: . . . . *(insert name of line manager)*

Department: . . . . *(insert name of department)*

Justification for the post *(insert whether this is a replacement, new post or an upgraded post)*:

Job description *(insert a description of the duties, responsibilities and level of seniority associated with the post)*:

Person specification *(insert a description of the level of qualifications, knowledge, skills, experience and competencies required for effective performance of the job)*:

Financial implications *(insert a proposed salary range, anticipated commencement date and any equipment requirements)*:

Media for publication and estimated advertising/recruitment costs:

Director's approval:
YES/NO

Director's comments:

Signed by line manager:
Date:

Signed by Director:
Date:

Please attach proposed advertisement wording.

JOB DESCRIPTION

Job title *(insert the name by which the job is usually known)*

. . . .

Department *(insert the section of the company where the post holder will be working)*

. . . .

Responsible to *(insert the job title of the line manager of this post)*

. . . .

Responsible for *(insert the job titles of any staff to be supervised by the post holder)*

. . . .

Job purpose *(insert a brief description of the role that this position covers)*

. . . .

Main duties *(insert a list of the main job duties. List and number them in order of importance)*

. . . .

. . . .

. . . .

Additional duties *(insert a list of other duties that the post holder may be required to undertake from time to time)*

. . . .

. . . .

. . . .

Main responsibilities *(insert a list of the post holder's responsibilities, including any delegated authority they may have)*

. . . .

. . . .

. . . .

Prepared by *(insert the name and job title of the person who prepared the job description)*

. . . .

Date *(insert the date for future reference)*

. . . .

The Company reserves the right to vary or amend the duties and responsibilities of the post holder at any time according to the needs of the Company's business.

PERSON SPECIFICATION

Qualities	Essential	Desirable
Physical make-up		
Height		
Build, strength		
Hearing		
Eyesight		
General health		
Dress		
Voice		
Attainments		
General education		
Job training		
Job experience		
General intelligence		
Tests		
General reasoning ability		
Special aptitudes		
Mechanical		
Manual dexterity		
Skill with words		
Skill with numbers		
Artistic ability		
Musical ability		
Interests		
Intellectual		
Practical/constructional		
Physically active		
Social/team player		
aesthetic		
Disposition		
Acceptability		
Leadership		
Stability		
Self-reliance		
Circumstances		
Age		
Mobility		
Domicile		

Date: . . . .

Prepared by: . . . .

APPLICATION FORM

Please complete this application form in black ink and then return it to ....

(insert name of contact).

Post applied for: ....

Personal Information

Surname:

Forenames:

Title (Mr, Mrs, Miss, Ms, etc.):

Previous names (if any):

Current address:

Daytime telephone number:

Do you have the right to take up   YES/NO
employment in the UK and, if necessary,
a Work Permit?

Dates you are **not** available for interview:

Education and Qualifications

From GCSE or equivalent to degree level in chronological order

From	**To**	**Establishment**	**Qualifications gained**

Postgraduate education or study or any other professional qualifications

From	**To**	**Establishment**	**Qualifications gained**

Employment history

Please give details of your last three jobs, beginning with your present or most recent. Any relevant posts held before then may also be mentioned.

From	To	Name and address of employer	Job title, description of duties and responsibilities, reason for leaving and salary on leaving.

Other Information

Do you hold a full driving licence? If yes, do you have any current endorsements?

Do you have any other training, qualifications or skills relevant to the post?

Please give details of any time not accounted for elsewhere on this application form.

Have you made a previous application to the Company? If so, when was this and what was the outcome?

Please use this space to say why you are interested in the post for which you have applied and provide any other information that may assist your application.

How many weeks' or months' notice do you have to give to your current employer?

If you are disabled, please give details of any special arrangements you would require to attend interview.

Referees

Please give details of two referees, one of whom should be your current or most recent employer. The other should not be a relative or contemporary.

First referee   **Second referee**

Declaration

I declare that the information I have given on this form is, to the best of my knowledge, true and complete. I understand that if it is subsequently discovered that any statement is false or misleading, or that I have withheld relevant information, my application may be disqualified or, if I have already been appointed, I may be dismissed. I hereby give my consent to the Company processing the data supplied on this application form for the purpose of recruitment and selection.

Signed: . . . .

Date: . . . .

ACKNOWLEDGEMENT OF APPLICATION LETTER

Date . . . . *(insert date of letter)*

Dear. . . . . *(insert name of job applicant)*

Re: Appointment of . . . . *(insert job title)*

Thank you for your application in respect of the above post.

We are currently in the process of assessing the applications received in order to produce a shortlist of applicants who will be invited for interview.

It is not the Company's policy to contact those applicants who have not been invited for interview so, if you have not heard from us by . . . . *(insert date)*, you should assume that, on this occasion, your application has not been successful.

OR

We will therefore contact you again shortly to let you know the outcome of your application.

In the meantime, we would like to thank you for the interest you have shown in our Company.

Yours sincerely,

. . . .

(Insert signature and name of author)

REJECTION OF UNSUCCESSFUL CANDIDATE
BEFORE INTERVIEW LETTER

Date . . . .*(insert date of letter)*

Dear . . . .*(insert name of job applicant)*

Re: Appointment of . . . . *(insert job title)*

Thank you for your application in respect of the above post.

We received a very good response to our advertisement and, having given careful consideration to your application, we regret to inform you that we have decided not to ask you to attend for an interview.

We would like to take this opportunity to thank you for expressing an interest in the post and in our Company and to wish you well in your search for suitable employment.

Yours sincerely,

. . . .
(Insert signature and name of author)

INVITATION TO ATTEND INTERVIEW LETTER

Date . . . . *(insert date of letter)*

Dear . . . . *(insert name of job applicant)*

Re: Appointment of . . . . *(insert job title)*

We refer to your recent application in respect of the above post.

Having given careful consideration to your application, we are pleased to advise you that we would like to invite you to attend an interview.

Your interview will be held on . . . . *(insert date)* at . . . .*(insert time)* at . . . . *(insert details of location)*. On arrival, you should ask for . . . . *(insert name of contact)*.

You will be interviewed by . . . . and . . . . *(insert names and job titles of interviewers)*. [In addition, you will be asked to undertake a selection test.] You will also be given a short tour of the Company's offices. We anticipate the interview process will take approximately . . . . *(insert duration)*.

If you are unable to attend this interview, could you please contact . . . . *(insert name of contact)* as a matter of urgency and we will endeavour to schedule an alternative appointment for you, although this cannot be guaranteed. If you have not already done so, please could you also let . . . . *(insert name of contact)* know if you require any special arrangements to be made for your interview on account of a disability or other ill-health problem.

We look forward to meeting you at interview. In the meantime, we enclose some information about our Company which you may find useful. You may also wish to take a look at our website at . . . . *(insert website address)*.

Yours sincerely,

. . . .

(Insert signature and name of author)

Encs.

REJECTION OF UNSUCCESSFUL CANDIDATE
AFTER INTERVIEW LETTER

Date . . . . *(insert date of letter)*

Dear . . . . *(insert name of job applicant)*

Re: Appointment of . . . . *(insert job title)*

Thank you for attending an interview on . . . . *(insert date)* in respect of the above post.

Having given careful consideration to your qualifications, experience and competencies for the position and your performance at interview [and in the selection test], when compared to other interviewees, we regret to inform you that your application has been unsuccessful on this occasion.

[We would, however, like to keep your personal details on file for a period of twelve months for future suitable vacancies. If you would prefer us not to hold your details, please contact . . . . *(insert name of contact)* and we will arrange to have them removed.]

We would like to take this opportunity to thank you for expressing an interest in the post and in our Company and to wish you well in your search for suitable employment.

Yours sincerely,

. . . .

(Insert signature and name of author)

OFFER OF APPOINTMENT LETTER

Date . . . . *(insert date of letter)*

Dear . . . . *(insert name of successful candidate)*

Re: Offer of appointment as . . . . *(insert job title)*

Further to your recent interview, we are pleased to offer you employment with the Company as . . . . *(insert job title)* on the following terms detailed below:

1. You will report to . . . . *(insert name of line manager)*.

2. Your starting salary will be £ . . . . *(insert amount)* per hour/week/annum payable weekly/monthly in arrears by credit transfer/cheque.

3. You will be entitled to . . . . *(insert number)* days' holiday each year [plus/including bank holidays].

4. Your normal hours of work will be from . . . . . *(insert time)* am to . . . . . *(insert time)* pm [Monday to Friday] with . . . . *(insert duration)* minutes/hour for lunch. [However, you may be required to work such additional hours (which may include weekends) as the needs of the business require. No extra payment will be made for this additional time/ Overtime at single time/time and a half/double time will be payable for hours worked over and above your normal working hours.]

Your employment will initially be on a . . . . *(insert duration)* months probationary period. During this time, the company will assess your performance and conduct and it reserves the right at any time during this period to terminate your employment with one/two week's/weeks' notice or payment in lieu, subject to compliance only with the statutory dismissal and disciplinary procedure. During this period, you are required to give one/two week's/weeks' notice if you wish to terminate your employment for whatever reason. Periods of notice thereafter are set out in the Statement of Employment Particulars. The company also reserves the right to extend your probationary period should it deem this necessary.

This offer of employment is conditional on the following documentation being obtained:

- two satisfactory references, one of which should be from your current or most recent employer
- [a Basic/Standard/Enhanced Certificate issued by the Criminal Records Bureau]
- [a satisfactory medical report]
- [proof of your stated qualifications/UK driving licence – please provide]
- evidence of your right to work in the UK – please provide an original document.

If you wish to accept this offer of employment, could you please telephone . . . . *(insert name of contact)* so that a start date can be agreed and the above matters discussed. Every effort will be made to obtain any required documentation as quickly as possible. Would you also sign the attached duplicate copy of this letter and return it to . . . . *(insert name of contact)*.

Full details of all your terms and conditions of employment are contained in the Statement of Employment Particulars and the Staff Handbook, copies of which will be provided to you within two months of your start date.

May we take this opportunity of welcoming you to the Company and we hope you will enjoy your career with us.

We look forward to hearing from you.

Yours sincerely,

. . . .
(Insert signature and name of author)

I accept the offer of employment on the terms set out in this conditional offer of appointment letter dated . . . . *(insert date)* and I hereby give my consent for you to contact my two referees, including my current employer.

Signed: . . . .

Date: . . . .

REFERENCE REQUEST

Date . . . . *(insert date of letter)*

Dear . . . . *(insert name of referee)*

Re: . . . . *(insert name of prospective employee)*

The person named above has applied for employment with our Company as a . . . . *(insert job title)* and has given your name as a referee . . . . *(insert name of prospective employee)* has agreed to us contacting you for the reference.

We would be grateful if you would comment on his/her *(delete as applicable)* suitability for the post by filling in the details below.

Job title: . . . .

Date of commencing employment: . . . .

Date of leaving employment: . . . .

Reason for leaving: . . . .

Final salary: . . . .

Summary of job duties: . . . .

. . . .

Competence in the job: . . . .

Ability to work without supervision: . . . .

Honesty/trustworthiness: . . . .

Attendance record: . . . .

Time-keeping record: . . . .

Relations with other work colleagues: . . . .

Disciplinary record: . . . .

Any other comments: . . . .

. . . .

Would you re-employ this person?. . . . . .Yes/No

If no, why not? . . . .

. . . .

Any information provided by you will be held in confidence, subject to the Data Protection Act 1998. A pre-paid envelope is enclosed for your convenience.

Yours sincerely,

. . . .

(Insert signature and name of author)

Encs.

RECRUITMENT POLICY

It is the Company's policy that line managers and the Human Resources department are jointly responsible for the recruitment of new employees. Line managers should always keep the senior management of the Company up-to-date regarding future recruitment intentions. Where there is a need to recruit a new employee into the Company, the following procedure should be followed:

1. The line manager should first complete a Recruitment Authorisation Form (copy attached) and ensure it is discussed with and signed off by a director of the Company. This form requires a justification for the post as well as:

   - an up-to-date job description and a person specification

   - financial implications

   - advertisement wording and medium for publication

   - estimated costs of advertising the post.

Where recruitment is planned to fill a vacancy created by a leaver (other than on redundancy grounds), approval will normally be granted automatically. If the post is new or upgraded, the director will need to be satisfied that it can be justified.

2. The form must then be forwarded to the Human Resources department for approval. If approved, they will deal with the necessary recruitment administration, including placing advertisements, arranging interviews, etc.

3. Selection of candidates for interview must be decided jointly by the line manager and the Human Resources department.

4. All interviews must be conducted by the line manager and at least one other line manager or member of the Human Resources department.

5. All offers of employment, whether written or verbal, must have the prior approval of a director of the Company.

It is the Company's policy that all vacancies will be advertised internally (by e-mail/posting on notice boards) as well as externally and existing employees are to be encouraged to apply for vacant posts if they have the requisite skills, qualifications and experience.

The Company aims at all times to recruit the person who is most suited to the particular post. Recruitment must be solely on the basis of the applicant's abilities, qualifications, experience and merit as measured against the job description and person specification. The guidelines promulgated in the Company's equal opportunities statement must be followed at all stages of recruitment and selection. Line managers conducting recruitment interviews must ensure that questions asked of job applicants are in no way discriminatory or personally intrusive. The interview should focus on the needs of the post and the skills, qualifications and experience needed to perform it effectively.

An interview record must be made and passed to the Human Resources department. On no account should a job offer be made during or at the end of an interview. Selection testing will be used as part of the recruitment process only with the prior approval of the Human Resources department. Any test used must have been validated in relation to the post and be conducted by a suitably trained person.

It is the Company's policy to seek at least two written references, one of which must be from a previous employer, and to ask for documentary proof of qualifications and eligibility to work in the UK. Any offer of employment must be conditional on this documentation being satisfactory to the Company. Before references are taken up, the prospective employee's consent should first be sought.

RELOCATION POLICY

Introduction

Relocation assistance is given by the Company to help with expenses incurred when an employee relocates as a result of employment with the Company. This generally occurs on joining the Company, although it can also occur if an employee changes office location during employment.

To be eligible for relocation assistance, an employee must be moving to a new home base either as a result of accepting the job with the Company or as a result of taking up a new position within the Company which is at a different office location to that where the employee is currently working. Relocation expenses are judged on a case-by-case basis and payment of them is entirely discretionary. Payment is not a contractual entitlement and, as such, may be varied or withdrawn at any time.

To be eligible for relocation assistance, the employee must be living more than . . . . *(insert number)* miles away from their new place of work/office location and must be moving to within . . . . *(insert number)* miles of their new place of work/office location. The employee must move to a permanent residence, which can either be purchased or rented.

House hunting

The Company will reimburse the reasonable travelling and overnight accommodation costs incurred by an employee or prospective employee in respect of a maximum of . . . . *(insert number)* visits to the area in connection with the purchase or rental of a new property, up to a maximum cost of £ . . . . *(insert amount)*.

Temporary accommodation

In circumstances where an employee has not been able to move home by the time they commence work at the Company or at the new office location, consideration will be given to the reimbursement of the costs of temporary accommodation. Typically, these take the form of bed and breakfasts or hotels. This type of accommodation will be allowed up to a maximum cost of £ . . . . *(insert amount)* per week and a maximum period of . . . . *(insert number)* weeks.

Buying and selling property

If approved, the Company will reimburse the following costs in the buying and selling of property to relocate:

- costs of selling an existing property, such as legal and estate agency fees, up to a maximum of £ . . . . *(insert amount)* including VAT
- costs of purchasing a new property, such as legal and survey fees, valuation and Land Registry fees up to a maximum of £ . . . . *(insert amount)* including VAT

- a contribution towards the Stamp Duty Land Tax incurred in connection with such purchase up to a maximum of £ . . . . *(insert amount)*
- removal and, if necessary, short-term storage costs including insurance up to a maximum of £ . . . . *(insert amount)* including VAT.

Moving to rented accommodation

If the employee has previously been living in rented accommodation before joining the Company and is intending to live in rented accommodation in the area, then relocation allowance is limited to the following:

- if approved, the Company will pay the deposit on the new rented accommodation. The deposit needs to be reimbursed to the Company within three months of moving to the property. The employee will be asked to sign a deposit agreement

- any associated administration costs from the lettings agent

- removal costs as detailed above in "buying and selling property".

Resettlement allowance

If approved, this allowance will only be paid once relocation has been completed for expenses incurred as a direct result of the move, such as the purchase of carpets and curtains. It covers any items the employee has needed to replace because of the disposal of the old home. Payment will be made up to a maximum of £ . . . . *(insert amount)*.

Authorisation

It is a condition of relocation assistance that all expenditure is supported by valid receipts and is incurred within . . . . *(insert number)* months of commencing employment with the Company/moving office location. Claim forms for repayment of relocation expenses can be obtained from . . . . *(insert name of contact)* and must be counter-signed by the employee's line manager.

Repayment of allowance

It is a condition of relocation expenses being paid that you agree to repay the Company a relevant proportion of them in the event that your employment with the Company terminates for whatever reason within two years. The relevant proportion is as follows:

Period of employment since taking up position requiring relocation:	Proportion repayable to the Company:
0 to twelve months	100%
Twelve months to two years	50%

By signing this policy, you also agree that the Company may deduct a sum up to or equal to the relocation expenses that you are required to repay from any outstanding wages that may be due from the Company to you on the termination of your employment. Any remaining amount due after termination must be repaid to the Company within one month of the date of your termination.

Signed: . . . . *(insert name of employee)*

Date: . . . .

EQUAL OPPORTUNITIES MONITORING FORM

In accordance with its equal opportunities statement, the Company will provide equal opportunities to all employees and job applicants and will not discriminate either directly or indirectly on the grounds of race, colour, ethnic origin, nationality, national origin, sex, marital status, disability, sexual orientation, religion or age.

In order to enable the Company ensure compliance with its policy statement, a system of monitoring has been set up. We have only asked for your name so that monitoring can take place both at the shortlisting for interview stage and at the appointment stage. Once an appointment has been made, the data given on this form will be stored on computer in an anonymised format and the form will then be destroyed.

You may, of course, decide not to answer one or any of these questions but if you do respond, all information provided will be treated in confidence and will be used solely by the Human Resources department for the purpose of providing statistics for equal opportunities monitoring. The monitoring form does not form part of your application and will therefore be detached from it on receipt and stored separately. You can always mail this form separately if you wish.

Thank you for your assistance in completing this form.

Name:	
Post title:	
Gender:	Male
	Female
	Prefer not to say
Marital status:	Married
	Single
	Other *(please specify)*
	Prefer not to say
Age band:	Under 18
	18 – 29
	30 – 39

	40 – 49	
	50 – 59	
	60 – 65	
	Over 65	
	Prefer not to say	
Sexual orientation:	Heterosexual	
	Homosexual	
	Bisexual	
	Transsexual	
	Prefer not to say	
Disabilities:	None	
	Physical disability	
	Mental disability	
	Prefer not to say	
Race/nationality/ ethnic origin:	White	English
		Scottish
		Welsh
		Irish
		British
		Other white background *(please specify)*
	Mixed	White and Black Caribbean
		White and Black African
		White and Black British
		White and Asian
		Other mixed background *(please specify)*

	Asian	Indian
		Pakistani
		Bangladeshi
		British
		Other Asian background *(please specify)*
	Black	Caribbean
		African
		British
		Other black background *(please specify)*
	Chinese	
	Other ethnic group *(please specify)*	
	Prefer not to say	
Religion:	Christian	
	Catholic	
	Jewish	
	Sikh	
	Muslim	
	Hindu	
	Buddhist	
	Rastafarian	
	None	
	Other religion *(please specify)*	
	Prefer not to say	

For the purposes of compliance with the Data Protection Act 1998, I hereby confirm that by completing this form I give my consent to the Company processing the data supplied on this form for the purpose of equal opportunities monitoring.

Signed: . . . .   Date: . . . .

Section II

Contracts of employment

Contracts of employment

Issuing at least a basic statement of the main terms and conditions of employment is a legal requirement. But the use of a full-blown contract with clauses tailored to suit your needs offers you far greater opportunities in terms of flexibility and control. However, there are pitfalls to watch out for.

LEGAL MINIMUM

As an absolute minimum, the law requires you to provide all employees taken on for one month or more with a written statement of employment particulars. You must do this within the first two months of service. Whilst there's no direct financial penalty for failing to do so, a tribunal is entitled to make a declaration as to what it thinks the main terms are - this might be very different to your interpretation! A sample **Written statement of employment particulars** is included at the back of this section. Use it if you want to ensure, as a minimum, you're legally safe. However, many employers prefer to issue a much more detailed contract (containing all of the statutory requirements of the written statement) plus a whole host of extras to suit the needs of the business. In essence you can bolt on whatever extras you need to - either to reward employees, e.g. through the use of bonus payments, or to restrict their post-employment activities (using restrictive covenants). In this section we've provided a selection of the most commonly requested contract clauses. It's by no means exhaustive but should at least form the basis of a very comprehensive employment contract. The other major benefit of a written agreement is that should there ever be a dispute between you and your staff over the terms they're employed under, the contract is much easier to prove if it's in writing.

SIGNATURE REQUIRED?

It's the age-old question - does the employee have to sign his contract for it to be enforceable? The simple answer is no. However, ideally it should be signed. If he refuses to sign find out what the problem is and take steps to resolve it.

However, if you still cannot obtain a signature, the longer the employee works for you without objecting to any terms of the contract, the more likely it will be that he's taken to have accepted them.

HOW TO USE THIS SECTION

We've included a selection of the most commonly requested contract clauses. What you need to do is ascertain which are most relevant to your workplace. Don't be tempted to include everything just for the sake of it. This will merely confuse staff and may lead to enforcement problems later. For example, if you never pay a bonus and don't intend to in the foreseeable future, don't include the **Bonus payment** clause - it could merely give staff the impression they're due something! Once you've made your selection you need to adapt the relevant clause to your requirements. For example, we'd recommend that most employers use a **Restrictive Covenant** of some description for senior or key employees. We've included six different types - so you need to choose which is most appropriate and amend it accordingly. As a general rule, remember that the greater the restriction, the less likely you'll be able to enforce it. Also think carefully about whether you're really protecting a legitimate business interest or seeking to punish an employee who goes to work for a competitor.

WHAT TO WATCH OUT FOR

There are several clauses that you really should consider using. If your business is subject to cyclical demand, a **Lay off and short-time working clause**. This enables you to lay staff off if you don't need them (and pay them just a statutory guarantee payment, maximum £17.80 per day at time of printing). Without such a clause you have to keep staff on at full pay - even if you don't have any work for them. Another useful clause is **Holiday pay on termination**. With this you're able to deduct any unearned but already paid annual leave from an employee's final salary payment. Finally, rather than be bogged down by your disciplinary warnings procedure for all staff, consider using the **Limiting disciplinary procedure** clause. This allows you to dismiss employees with less than twelve months' service without having to slavishly follow all the warnings. Unfortunately, you will still need to follow the new statutory dismissal and disciplinary procedures, details of which are set out in the clause.

CHANGING TERMS

If you'd like to use several of the clauses in this section, is it as simple as adding them to the existing contract of staff? Well it might be if they're better off as a result. But the reality is that it's not always so simple. It's unlawful for you to unilaterally change an existing employee's contract of employment without his agreement - unless the change is permitted by the contract itself. To impose contractual changes without his express agreement constitutes a breach of contract. If the breach is sufficiently serious and the employee has one or more years' service, he may then claim that he's been constructively unfairly dismissed if he's forced to resign due to your actions. So, inform the employee both verbally and in writing that you're proposing (not making) a change. You should set out in detail the nature of the proposed change and why you think it is so important. The employee should be invited to consider the change and revert to you with his views. If he's willing to accept the change, it can then be incorporated into his contract of employment and, for the avoidance of doubt, his consent to it should be obtained in writing. This can usefully be done by issuing a new contract for the employee to sign.

BUT WHAT IF THE EMPLOYEE REFUSES TO CO-OPERATE?

There are three possible options. The first is that the employee is not willing to accept the proposed change but you nevertheless impose it on him in breach of contract. The second is that you terminate the employee's current contract of employment and then offer to re-engage him on new terms and conditions. The final option is that you forget all about implementing the change - which is always the safest course of action, but this may not help your business needs! You run the risk that, if your breach of contract is sufficiently serious or fundamental, the employee will resign and then claim constructive dismissal before an employment tribunal (if he has one or more years' service). Fundamental breaches include things like reductions in wages and working hours and probably changes to work location. Even if he doesn't resign, your employee can still claim damages for breach of contract against you in the county court. Of course your employee might not resign or claim breach of contract. He might simply do nothing. If he's not willing to accept a proposed change but you impose it on him anyway, if he then continues to work under the new terms without making his objections known to you, after a period of time (usually months rather than weeks) he could be deemed to have accepted the change. It would then be incorporated into his contract of employment. Exactly how long an employee must work before being taken to have impliedly agreed to a contract variation depends on the facts of each case. Whatever the situation, the principle of deemed acceptance probably only applies to those provisions of the contract that are operative on a day-to-

day basis where the variation has an obvious effect. For example, this might mean that a purported change to the notice of termination provisions cannot be subject to the principle of deemed acceptance. This is because this clause only really comes into operation when either the employee resigns or you terminate his employment. The clause does not operate on a day-to-day basis. Clauses that clearly do operate on a day-to-day basis are those relating to hours of work, annual leave and pay.

Alternatively, the employee could work under the new terms and conditions under protest, in which case there is no acceptance by him meaning you are still in breach of contract. In this case, you can expect the employee to expressly state that he is working under protest because he does not accept the change. Note that there will be a limit on the time he can continue to work under protest and keep open the option of resigning and claiming constructive dismissal. He cannot work under protest forever! Each case will turn on its own facts and circumstances.

CONTRACTUAL AGREEMENTS

At the end of the section are four standalone agreements. They should be used as and when needed. For example you should ask staff to sign the **Opt-out agreement** if you want them to work for more than 48 hours per week. Similarly the **Training costs agreement** is essential if you're investing in staff training and worried that they might leave as soon as they've achieved their certificate or whatever. Without our agreement you could be considerably out of pocket. But do note that it must be signed before commencement of the training.

BONUS PAYMENT

The Company may, from time to time and depending on its performance and your overall performance and conduct, pay you a bonus. The payment or otherwise of any bonus will be wholly at the discretion of the Company. There is no contractual entitlement for you to receive a bonus at any time even if a bonus has been paid to you or to other employees on previous occasions. If a bonus is paid the amount will also be wholly at the discretion of the Company.

CONFIDENTIALITY

You agree that you will not use, divulge or communicate to any person, firm or organisation (and in the course of your business) any of the trade secrets or other confidential, technical or commercial information of the Company relating to the business, organisation, accounts, analysis or other affairs of the Company's which you may have received or obtained while working for the Company. This includes;

1. Any information relating to the trading position of the Company including in particular names of clients or customers.

2. Any document or item marked as confidential.

This restriction will continue to apply after the termination of your employment but will cease to apply to any information which may come into the public domain through disclosure by the Company.

DEDUCTIONS FROM WAGES

If you leave without giving the proper period of notice or leave during your notice period without consent, the Company will be entitled to a day's pay for each day not worked during the notice period. This is on the understanding that the Company will not deduct a sum in excess of the actual loss suffered by it as a result of your leaving without notice. Any sum so deducted will be in full and final settlement of the Company's claim for your breach of contract. The deduction will be made from any final payment of salary which the Company may be due to make to you. Note that the amount deducted is a genuine attempt by the Company to assess its loss as a result of your leaving without notice and is not intended to act as a penalty.

DEMOTION AS A DISCIPLINARY SANCTION

Here are two examples of clauses that can be adapted for use in your own employment contracts. The first is to be used in a punitive way where the employee has a misconduct or attendance problem. The second is for use where the employee's work is below par.

1. Where disciplinary action is for your misconduct or poor attendance, as an alternative to issuing a formal written warning or as an alternative to dismissal, the Company reserves the right to demote you for a fixed period, but for no longer than three months. This will be done by notice in writing to you. The Company also reserves the right to impose a reduction in your pay for the period of demotion and the written notice will detail any changes to your terms and conditions of employment arising from such demotion. In particular the notice will give details of any reduction to your salary and/or loss of benefits arising from the demotion.

2. Where disciplinary action is for your poor standard of work or your failure to meet required standards of performance, as an alternative to issuing a formal written warning or as an alternative to dismissal, the Company reserves the right to demote you for such period as is necessary to enable you to reach the desired standards. This period shall not exceed six months and will be reviewed by the Company every month. The Company also reserves the right to impose a reduction in your pay for the period of the demotion and the written notice will detail any changes to your terms and conditions of employment arising out of the demotion. In particular the notice will give details of any reduction to your salary and/or loss of benefits arising from the demotion.

FLEXIBILITY CLAUSE

The Company's normal hours of work are from . . . . *(insert hours)*, ... *(insert days)* with . . . . *(insert minutes)* break for lunch. These hours will be your normal hours of work unless otherwise agreed between you and the Company. You may be required to work such additional hours as are reasonably necessary for the proper performance of your duties. [No extra payment will be made for any additional hours worked, unless expressly authorised by your line manager.] or [Any overtime worked by you at the request of the Company will be paid at the rate of £ . . . *(insert figure)* per hour.] or [. . . *(insert figure)* times your normal hourly rate.]

FLEXIBLE JOB DUTIES

There will be times when you may be required to undertake additional tasks, duties and responsibilities within your capabilities and will be asked to transfer to an alternative job. Where this is agreed on a permanent basis it will be confirmed to you in writing. However, you will not be assigned to duties or required to perform services which you cannot reasonably perform or are outside the range of your normal skills and experience.

GARDEN LEAVE

The Company reserves the right to ask you not to attend work at any time at its sole discretion. During any period that you are not required to work, you will continue to be employed by the Company and will continue to receive your normal pay and benefits. In particular, if you give notice to terminate your contract or if the Company gives you notice to terminate you may be asked not to attend work during any or all of the notice period. In such circumstances, your employment will continue throughout the notice period and you will remain bound by all the terms of your contract. You will, therefore, not be entitled to perform any work for any other employer until your notice period has expired and your employment is formally terminated.

HOLIDAY PAY ON TERMINATION

On termination of your employment, you will be paid for holiday not taken in that year. If, on termination, you have taken more holiday than you have earned in that year, the Company shall be entitled as a result of your agreement to the terms of this contract to deduct the value of the unearned holiday from any final payment of salary made to you. Holiday pay will be at a rate derived from annual salary accruing at . . . *(insert number)* of days per months.

HOLIDAY SHUTDOWN

.... *(insert number of days)* of your annual holiday entitlement must be taken [e.g. during the off-peak summer months/at Christmas] when the Company operates a shutdown. The Company will give you notice of the exact dates you are required to take as annual leave as early as possible after the start of the holiday year and in any event at least one month in advance of the shutdown.

INTELLECTUAL PROPERTY

Where the employee makes or creates any intellectual property rights which may be of benefit to the Company, he or she shall inform the Company immediately in writing. These intellectual property rights will then be owned absolutely by the Company. The employee shall co-operate fully to ensure such ownership and in so doing waives all moral rights to them.

Alternatively, you could use:

The employee makes or creates intellectual property rights in the course of his duties set out in clause ... *(insert number)* of this contract of employment and, as a special obligation to further the interests of the Company's business in this respect.

Note. Intellectual property rights means patents, copyright, registered and unregistered design rights, trademarks, plant variety rights and any other intellectual property rights throughout the world, applications for registration of any of the same, confidential information and know how whether registered or unregistered.

LAY OFF AND SHORT-TIME WORKING

The Company reserves the right to lay you off or put you on short-time working where the needs of the Company's business makes this necessary. You will be paid guaranteed payments at the prevailing statutory rate during any period of lay off or short-time working.

LIMITING DISCIPLINARY PROCEDURE

The disciplinary procedure will apply only to employees who have . . . . . . *(insert figure, usually twelve)* months' continuous service at the date of the commission of any offence. Employees with less service who commit an offence or whose performance falls below the standard required may be liable, at the management's discretion, to dismissal where appropriate in accordance with the following non-contractual procedure:

Stage 1: Notification of allegations. The Company will notify the employee in writing of the allegations against him and will invite the employee to a disciplinary meeting to discuss the matter. The Company will also notify the employee of the basis for the complaint of alleged misconduct or poor performance.

Stage 2: Disciplinary meeting. Having given the employee a reasonable opportunity to consider his response to the allegations, a disciplinary meeting will then take place at which the employee will be given the chance to state his case. The employee may be accompanied if requested by a trade union official or a fellow employee of his choice. The employee must take all reasonable steps to attend that meeting. Following the meeting, the employee will be informed of the Company's decision in writing and notified of his right to appeal against it.

Stage 3: Appeals. If the employee wishes to appeal against the Company's decision, he can do so within five working days of the decision. Appeals should be made in writing and state the grounds for appeal. The employee will be invited to attend an appeal meeting chaired by a more senior manager. At the appeal meeting, the employee will again be given the chance to state his case and will have the right to be accompanied by a trade union official or a fellow employee of his choice. Following the appeal meeting, the employee will be informed of the appeal decision in writing. The Company's decision on an appeal will be final.

LIST OF GROSS MISCONDUCT OFFENCES

For gross misconduct, the Company reserves the right to summarily dismiss an employee and normally dismissal will be without notice with pay only up to the point of dismissal.

Examples of gross misconduct where the Company has reasonable grounds for believing that the following matters have occurred are:

- dishonesty, theft or fraud

- communicating confidential information to third parties

- working for a competitor without permission

- falsification of company records or unauthorised removal or sale of company products or property

- wilful damage to company property

- conviction of a serious criminal offence (taking into account the provisions of the Rehabilitation of the Offenders Act 1974)

- taking bribes in connection with employment

- actions which endanger an employee's safety

- knowingly breaking a legal requirement in connection with employment

- assault or threatening, inflammatory behaviour or rudeness to customers

- gross insubordination

- wilful refusal to carry out reasonable and proper requests

- false expense claims for fraudulent purposes

- being under the influence of alcohol or illegal drugs during working hours or on company property

- unauthorised absence.

This list is not exhaustive and can be added to suit the particular needs of each employer.

MEDICAL EXAMINATIONS

The Company may require you to undergo a medical examination by a medical practitioner at any stage of your employment. The cost of any such examination will be met by the Company and you will co-operate in the disclosure of all results and reports to the Company. The Company will only request such an examination where reasonable to do so but your failure to co-operate without justifiable reason may result in disciplinary action being taken.

MOBILITY/RELOCATION

The Company reserves the right to require the employee to work at such other place of business of the Company (or of its associated Companies) (within . . . . *(insert figure in miles)*/reasonable commuting distance of the employees' home within the United Kingdom), as the employer may from time to time reasonably require whether on a temporary or permanent basis on giving . . . *(insert figure e.g. a week's prior written notice)* to the employee of such requirement.

OUTSIDE BUSINESS INTERESTS

You are expected to devote your whole time, skill and attention during working hours to your work for the Company.

You must not engage in any other work outside working hours, paid or unpaid, without the prior permission of your manager. Permission will not be granted for you to engage in any activity that the company believes to be direct or indirect competition with the Company's business or which in the Company's view does or might impair your ability to perform your duties for the Company fully and efficiently.

PAY IN LIEU OF NOTICE

The Company reserves the right to make a payment in lieu of notice for all or any part of your notice period on the termination of your employment. This provision, which is at the Company's discretion, applies whether notice to terminate the contract is given by you or the Company. Any such payment will consist solely of basic salary and shall be subject to such deductions of income tax and National Insurance contributions as the Company is required or authorised to make.

PROBATION PERIOD

Your employment by the Company is subject to a probation period of . . . . . *(insert suitable figure e.g. one, two or three months)* during which time you will be required to demonstrate your suitability for the position in which you are employed. To this end progress will be assessed on a regular basis. The probation period may be extended at the Company's discretion . . . . *(insert figure e.g. maximum of six months)* and is without prejudice to the Company's right to terminate your employment before the expiry of the probation period.

During the probation period the notice period will be . . . . . *(insert figure e.g. one week)* and the Company's disciplinary procedure will not apply to you. The Company will only be obliged to follow the statutory dismissal and disciplinary procedure as set out in the Limiting Disciplinary Procedure clause.

RESTRICTIVE COVENANTS

Note: Before inserting a restrictive covenant of any type into an employee's contract of employment, you must always consider whether it is really necessary to protect a legitimate business interest. If you do have a legitimate business interest to protect in relation to the particular employee, consider whether this can be achieved by a non-solicitation, non-dealing, non-poaching and / or a non-competition clause. Always remember that the shorter the duration of the covenant and the more limited it is in scope, the more likely it will be enforceable.

In order to protect the Company's interest in its goodwill and business connections, you hereby undertake that:

1. **Non-dealing.** You shall not at any time prior to the termination of your employment either on your own behalf or for any other person directly or indirectly approach, canvass, solicit or otherwise endeavour to entice away from the Company the custom of any person who is a customer, client or supplier of the Company and you shall not use your knowledge of or influence over any such customer, client or supplier to or for your own benefit or for the benefit of any other person carrying on business in competition

with the Company or otherwise use your knowledge of or influence over any such customer, client or supplier to the detriment of the Company;

2. **Non-poaching.** You shall not at any time prior to the termination of your employment either on your own behalf or for any other person directly or indirectly endeavour to entice away from the Company, any person who is an employee of the Company or otherwise encourage any such employee to breach his contract of employment;

3. **Non-solicitation.** You shall not for a period of . . . . *(insert figure)* months after the termination of your employment either on your own behalf or for any other person directly or indirectly approach, canvass, solicit or otherwise endeavour to entice away from the Company the custom of any person or company who at any time during the . . . . *(insert figure)* months preceding the termination of your employment both has been a customer, client or supplier of the Company and with whom you shall have personally had dealings;

4. **Non-dealing.** You shall not for a period of . . . . *(insert figure)* months after the termination of your employment either on your own behalf or for any other person supply, directly or indirectly and whether solicited by you or not, any goods or services to any person or company who at any time during the . . . . *(insert figure)* months preceding the termination of your employment both has been a customer, client or supplier of the Company and with whom you shall have personally had dealings;

5. **Non-poaching.** You shall not for a period of . . . . *(insert figure)* months after the termination of your employment either on your own behalf or for any other person directly or indirectly approach, canvass, solicit or otherwise endeavour to entice away any person who shall be an employee of the Company at the date of termination of your employment and with whom you had regular contact with during the . . . . *(insert figure)* months preceding the termination of your employment with a view to the specific knowledge or skills of such person being used by or for the benefit of any person carrying on business in competition with the business carried on by the Company;

6. **Non-competition.** You shall not for a period of . . . . *(insert figure)* months after the termination of your employment either on your own behalf or on behalf of or in association with any other person directly or indirectly be engaged, concerned or interested as an employee or in any other capacity in any business [within . . . . *(insert figure)* miles radius of . . . . *(insert a specific point)*] [within . . . . *(insert a defined area)*] where you would be acting in direct competition with that part of the business carried on at the date of termination of your employment by the Company with which you were involved as an employee in the . . . . *(insert figure)* months prior to the termination of your employment. That part of the business is defined as . . . . *(insert specific nature of business in which employee was personally involved)*.

Always add this to whichever clause you use: Each sub-clause of this clause constitutes an entirely separate and independent restriction on you. Where any sub-clause of this clause is held void or unlawful or unenforceable in any respect then such sub-clause shall be severed from this Contract without prejudice to the validity or enforcement of the other sub-clauses of this Contract.

RETURN OF COMPANY PROPERTY

On termination of your employment, for whatever reason, the employee will return to the Company all documents, software, hardware, credit or charge cards, Company car and any other property belonging to the Company. The employee also undertakes to return to the Company forthwith any such property that may come into his/her possession or control after the termination of his/her employment.

SICK PAY

You are entitled to Statutory Sick Pay (SSP) during periods of properly certified sickness absence. Details of the SSP scheme can be obtained from . . . . *(insert details)*. Any payment over and above SSP rates will be paid at the absolute discretion of the Company. Notwithstanding the Company's discretion, it does operate an occupational sick pay scheme.

This scheme will, in normal circumstances, provide you with up to a total of *(insert figure)* weeks at full pay and . . . . *(insert figure)* weeks at . . . . *(insert percentage figure)* of pay during any periods of properly certified sickness absence in any period of 365 days. Thereafter within the same period within 365 days the Company may provide further payments to you during sickness absence but it is under no obligation to do so. Any such sick pay will be deemed to include your entitlement to SSP.

SUSPENSION CLAUSE

Where an allegation of serious misconduct is involved, you may be immediately suspended from work on full pay and contractual benefits. Any decision to suspend will be confirmed in writing within . . . . *(insert figure, e.g. three)* working days and such written confirmation will state that the nature of the suspension is precautionary, not disciplinary, pending the outcome of the disciplinary proceedings. Suspension is a neutral act which does not imply guilt or blame and will be for as short a period as possible.

TRAINING COSTS AGREEMENT

THIS AGREEMENT is dated 2004

AND IS MADE BETWEEN:-

. . . . *("the Employee")*; and

. . . . *("the Employer")*.

WHEREAS:-

A. The Employee is employed by the Employer as a *(insert grade / job title)*.

B. The Employee has obtained a place in relation to a course of study leading to the award of . . . . *(insert name of qualification)* in . . . . *(insert subject)* at . . . . *(insert name of college / institute of further or higher education)* ("the Course").

IT IS HEREBY AGREED AND DECLARED THAT

1. In consideration of the Employer agreeing to meet the costs of the Course which are set out in the Schedule to this Agreement ("the Costs"), the Employee undertakes to reimburse to the Employer the Costs if:

   (i) he voluntarily withdraws from or terminates the Course early without the Employer's prior written consent;

   (ii) he is dismissed or otherwise compulsorily discharged from the Course, unless the dismissal or discharge arises out of the discontinuance generally of the Course;

   (iii) his employment is terminated by the Employer for any reason prior to completion of the Course; or

   (iv) he resigns from the employment of the Employer either prior to completion of the Course or within (two years/twelve months) after the end of the Course, except that, in the latter case, the amount which would otherwise be due to the Employer shall be reduced by [1/24th/1/12th] part for each complete calendar month after the end of the Course during which the Employee remains employed by the Employer.

2. To the extent permitted by law, the Employee agrees that the Employer may deduct a sum equal to the whole or part of the Costs due under the terms of this Agreement from his wages (as defined in section 27 of the Employment Rights Act 1996) or from any other allowances, expenses or other payments due to the Employee.

3. The amount due to the Employer under the terms of this Agreement is a genuine attempt by the Employer to assess its loss as a result of the termination of the Employee's employment and takes into account the derived benefit to the Employer. This Agreement is not intended to act as a penalty on the Employee upon termination of his employment.

Signed:

....

(insert name of employee)

Signed:

....

(insert name of manager)

for and on behalf of *(insert name of employer)*

NB. This Agreement must be signed by both parties prior to the commencement of the Course.

SCHEDULE

(Insert details of the costs to be incurred by the Employer in relation to the Course e.g. the Course fees, examination fees, the costs of books or other materials, any other expenses paid in connection with the Course.)

FIXED TERM CONTRACT

This Statement dated . . . . . . *(insert date)* sets out details of the main terms of your employment with . . . . *(insert Company name)*, which are required to be given to you under the Employment Rights Act 1996.

Employee:

. . . . *(insert name of employee).*

Commencement of Employment:

Your employment with the Company commenced on . . . . *(insert date)*. No previous employment counts toward your period of continuous employment with the Company.

Job Title:

The title of the job which you are employed to do is: . . . . *(insert job title).*

The Company may amend your duties from time to time, and, in addition to your normal duties you may from time to time be required to undertake additional or other duties as necessary to meet the needs of the business.

Duration of Employment:

Your employment is on a fixed term basis, and is currently expected to continue only until . . . . . . *(insert date)*. Your employment is subject to termination by either party giving the notice specified later in this statement.

Place of work:

Your usual place of work is . . . . *(insert address).*

Pay:

Your pay is £ . . . . (insert figure).

Hours of work:

Your hours of work are . . . . *(insert hours).*

Holidays:

Your holiday entitlement is .... *(insert number of days)*.

Additional holiday rules are set out in the Employee Handbook.

Sick Pay:

If you are absent from work because of sickness or injury you will be entitled to Statutory Sick Pay, provided you meet the qualifying conditions. Further details about sick pay are set out in the Employee Handbook.

Pension:

The Company operates a stakeholder pension scheme which you may be entitled to join. Full details of the scheme can be obtained from .... *(insert details)*.

Notice:

During the first month of your employment, either the Company or you may give 24 hours' notice to terminate your employment.

After one month's continuous service, you are entitled to receive the following notice of termination of employment from the Company:

More than one month but less than two years' continuous service:	One week
More than two years' continuous service:	One week for each complete year of service up to a maximum of twelve weeks after twelve years' service.

The Company reserves the right to make payment in lieu of notice.

Disciplinary Rules and Procedure:

The Disciplinary Procedure applicable to you is set out in the Employee Handbook. You are strongly advised to read it.

Appeal Procedure:

If you are dissatisfied with any disciplinary decision taken in respect of you, you may appeal to .... *(insert details)*. Further details of the appeal procedure are set out in Disciplinary Procedure section of the Employee Handbook.

Grievance Procedure:

The Grievance Procedure applicable to you is set out in the Employee Handbook.

Acknowledgement:

I acknowledge receipt of this statement. I confirm that I have read the statement and the Employee Handbook which set out the principal rules, policies and procedures relating to my employment.

Signed: . . . .

Print name: . . . .

Dated: . . . .

OPT-OUT AGREEMENT

I, ... *(insert name of employee)* agree with ....
.... *(insert name of employer)* that:

1. the 48-hour weekly working time limit under the Working Time Regulations does not apply to me

2. this agreement applies for .... *(specify a fixed period or that it applies indefinitely)* and

3. this agreement is terminable by me giving .... *(specify a period of notice of up to three months)* notice in writing to the employer.

I have read and understood all of the above and freely give my agreement to it.

Signed: ....

Print Name: ....

Dated: ....

WRITTEN STATEMENT OF EMPLOYMENT PARTICULARS

1. You . . . . *(insert name)* began employment with . . . . *(insert Company name)* on . . . . *(insert start date).* No previous service will count towards your continuous service with . . . . *(insert Company name).*

2. Your job title is . . . .

3. You will work at . . . .

4. You are required/permitted to work at . . . . *(insert location)* and the address of your employer is . . . . *(insert address).*

5. Your pay will be . . . . *(insert figure).*

6. You will be paid . . . . *(insert monthly, weekly etc.).*

7. Your hours of work are . . . .

8. Your holiday entitlement is . . . .

9. In case of incapacity for work . . . . *(insert details of any sick pay scheme you operate or refer to a document giving full details).*

10. Pension scheme particulars [if relevant].

11. The amount of notice of termination of your employment you are entitled to receive is . . . . and the amount you are required to give is . . . .

12. Your employment is permanent [or, if relevant give temporary/fixed-term details].

13. The collective agreements which directly affect your employment are . . . .

14. The disciplinary rules and procedure that apply to you are . . . . *(insert details or make reference to a document where they can be found).*

15. If you are unhappy with any disciplinary decision that affects you, you should appeal in accordance with the appeal procedure which is . . . . *(insert details or make reference to a document where the appeal procedure can be found).*

16. The grievance procedure that applies to you is . . . . *(insert details or make reference to a document where it can be found).*

Section III

Company rules and
staff handbooks

Company rules and staff handbooks

In addition to issuing a contract of employment or a written statement of employment particulars, it's best practice to issue a series of standalone company rules and policies or a staff handbook containing these documents. So what's involved?

STAFF HANDBOOK

You know that you're obliged to provide a statement of employment particulars to all employees within two months of their starting work for you. In fact, you will probably provide a more detailed contract of employment containing additional clauses to give you extra protection as an employer. Section II provides further information and precedent clauses for use in drafting contracts of employment. On top of this documentation, a good employer will also provide a staff handbook. This will take account of the main statutory rights that employees have (for example, maternity, flexible working, time off for dependants, equal opportunities and dignity at work), as well as providing details of the Company's rules and procedures on a variety of matters, such as the provision of a car, health and safety, personal relationships at work and the use of company equipment. The advantage of a staff handbook over a series of standalone rules and policies is that the employee knows precisely where to look and where he or she stands, particularly if the handbook is kept updated.

The particular rules, statements or policies that should be included in your staff handbook depend on the requirements of your business. The precedents contained in this section have been drafted so that you can select which ones are appropriate for you and can then put them together to form a comprehensive staff handbook. In practice, the staff handbook will be more voluminous than the statement of employment particulars/contract of employment itself. We hope you will be able to find a suitable precedent in this section to cover the employment situation with which you are concerned, but please be aware that it's not possible to draft precedents to cover every single eventuality.

CONTRACTUAL EFFECT

If you intend all the provisions in the staff handbook to be definitively binding on your employees, you should refer to it as expressly forming part of the employees' contracts of employment and then make reference to the handbook in the statement of employment particulars/contract of employment. Finally, you should ensure that all staff are given a copy of the handbook and ask them to sign a short statement to confirm they have received, read and understood its contents and that they agree to its provisions. Otherwise, you are at risk that the provisions in the staff handbook may be held not to be contractually binding, in which case clauses such as those relating to deductions from wages may not be enforceable. On the other hand, if the handbook is contractual, note that this means you may not unilaterally vary its substantive terms and you will need the express agreement of the employees (see Section VII on Changing Terms and Conditions of Employment). You will not, however, need employees' agreement to make minor procedural changes or to make changes which reflect recent developments in the law.

Another possible option would be to divide the staff handbook into two sections: a section covering those provisions that do not have contractual effect and a section containing those provisions that are to have contractual effect. In deciding what to put in each section, bear in mind that, in strict employment law terms, a statement of policy or a statement of company rules is generally only classed as having contractual effect when it may be regarded as conferring rights on employees. If it simply lays down standards of good practice which an employee or employer would be expected to follow, it will probably not have contractual effect.

ADOPTION LEAVE

The Company implements the adoption leave rights set out in legislation.

In order to qualify for the right to take adoption leave, you must be adopting a child through an approved adoption agency and you must have worked for the Company for a continuous period of 26 weeks calculated as at the week in which you are notified by the adoption agency of having been matched with the child for adoption.

If you are jointly adopting a child with your spouse or partner, only one of you will be entitled to take adoption leave. You can choose which adopter will take adoption leave. The other adoptive parent will normally be entitled to take paternity leave, provided they meet the relevant eligibility criteria (see the section on Paternity Leave).

The right to adoption leave is not available to foster parents who adopt a child they are fostering, nor to step-parents who adopt their partner's child.

Statutory adoption pay

During adoption leave, most employees will be entitled to Statutory Adoption Pay. The rate of Statutory Adoption Pay is £102.80 per week or a rate equivalent to 90% of your average weekly earnings if this is less than £102.80 per week. Employees who earn less than the lower earnings limit for National Insurance purposes are not eligible to receive Statutory Adoption Pay.

Statutory Adoption Pay is paid into your bank account in the same way as salary is normally paid and it is subject to deductions of income tax and National Insurance contributions.

Adoption leave

Assuming you are eligible, you are able to take up to a maximum of 52 weeks' adoption leave. This comprises 26 weeks' ordinary adoption leave and 26 weeks' additional adoption leave.

Ordinary adoption leave

During ordinary adoption leave, your contract of employment continues and you are entitled to receive all your contractual benefits, except for salary. This means, for example, that holiday entitlement will continue to accrue. This also includes other benefits such as: pension contributions, private medical insurance, life assurance and permanent health insurance.

You should endeavour to take any outstanding annual leave that may be due to you before the commencement of your adoption leave and you are reminded that annual leave must be taken in the holiday year in which it is earned: see the section on Holidays for further information.

Additional adoption leave

Additional adoption leave starts immediately after the end of ordinary adoption leave and continues for a further 26 weeks. Your contract of employment continues during additional adoption leave but only some terms of the contract will continue. The terms and conditions which apply during additional adoption leave are:

- you are entitled to benefit from the Company's implied obligation of trust and confidence

- you are bound by your implied obligation to the Company of good faith

- you are entitled to receive your contractual notice period if your employment is terminated

- you must give the Company the notice provided for in your contract if you wish to terminate your employment

- the terms and conditions in your contract of employment relating to disciplinary and grievance procedures will continue to apply

- you are bound by the terms in your contract relating to disclosure of confidential information and participation in any other business.

During additional adoption leave, entitlement to statutory annual leave under the **Working Time Regulations 1998** will continue to accrue, but all further contractual annual leave entitlement (including entitlement to paid bank holidays) will cease. Contractual annual leave accrual will recommence when you return to work after additional adoption leave.

Commencing adoption leave: notice requirements

If you wish to take adoption leave, you must inform your line manager in writing of your request no later than seven days after the date on which notification of the match with the child is provided to you by the adoption agency. You must provide written details of the date on which you were notified of having been matched with the child, the date the child is expected to be placed with you for adoption and when you want your adoption leave to start. An Adoption Leave Request Form can be obtained from . . . . *(insert name of contact)*. As evidence of your entitlement to adoption leave, you will also be required to provide a copy of the matching certificate and adoption papers from the adoption agency.

You are permitted to change your mind about when you want to start your adoption leave providing you give the Company at least 28 days' written notice of the revised start date.

Once you have notified your adoption leave plans, the Company will write to you within 28 days, setting out the date on which we expect you to return to work if you take your full entitlement to adoption leave.

Adoption leave can start on the day the child is placed with you for adoption or on a date which is up to 14 days before the expected date of placement.

Returning to work after adoption leave: notice requirements

You may simply return on your due day of return. That said, if you want to return after the end of ordinary adoption leave, you must still give us 28 days' notice. If you fail to give the appropriate notice, we may postpone your return to such a date as will give the Company 28 days' notice, provided that this is not later than the end of your additional adoption leave.

If you are unable to attend work at the end of your adoption leave due to sickness or injury, the Company's normal arrangements for sickness absence will apply.

If you do not intend to return to work at all after your adoption leave, you are still required to give the Company written notice of the termination of your employment as set out in your contract of employment.

Your rights on return to work

On resuming work after ordinary adoption leave, you are entitled to return to the same job on the same terms and conditions as if you had not been absent. On resuming work after additional adoption leave, again you are entitled to return to the same job on the same terms and conditions as if you had not been absent. If, however, there is some reason why it is not reasonably practicable for the Company to take you back in your original job, you will be offered suitable alternative work of equivalent status and responsibility.

Adoptions from overseas

If you adopt a child from overseas, you may still be entitled to statutory adoption leave and pay. Special rules apply in these circumstances. For further information, please contact . . .
. . . . (insert name of contact).

ALCOHOL AND DRUGS

Alcohol and drug misuse or abuse can be a serious problem within the workplace. Employees who drink excessively or take unlawful drugs are more likely to work inefficiently, be absent from work, have work accidents and endanger their colleagues. The Company has a duty to protect the health, safety and welfare of all its employees. However, the Company recognises that, for a number of reasons, employees could develop alcohol or drug related problems. In relation to drugs, these rules apply to those that are unlawful under the criminal law and not to prescribed medication. These rules aim to promote a responsible attitude to drink and drugs and to offer assistance to employees who may need it.

Advice and counselling

It is the Company's intention to deal constructively and sympathetically with an employee's alcohol or drug related problems, such as alcohol or drug dependency. When it is known that an employee has an alcohol or drug problem . . . . *(insert name of contact),* will be able to provide advice and guidance on how to seek suitable treatment. The primary objective of any discussions will be to assist the employee with the problem in as compassionate and constructive a way as possible. Any discussions of the nature of an employee's alcohol or drug problem and the record of any treatment will be strictly confidential unless the employee agrees otherwise.

If you have an alcohol or drug problem, you should seek appropriate help. If you have an alcohol or drug problem which affects your conduct or performance at work and you refuse the opportunity to receive help, the matter will be referred for action under the Company's disciplinary procedure as appropriate. Likewise, if after accepting counselling and assistance, and following review and evaluation, your conduct or work performance reverts to the problem level, the matter may also be dealt with through the disciplinary procedure.

Prohibition on alcohol and drug consumption in the workplace

No alcohol or drugs must be brought onto or consumed on Company premises at any time. Staff must never drink alcohol or take drugs if they are required to drive private or Company vehicles on Company business. Staff must also not drink alcohol or take drugs when they are on operational standby or on call.

Employees representing the Company at business/client functions or conferences or attending Company organised social events outside normal working hours are expected to be moderate if drinking alcohol and to take specific action to ensure they are well within the legal limits if they are driving. They are prohibited from taking drugs on these occasions.

Social drinking after normal working hours and away from the Company's premises is, of course, generally a personal matter and does not directly concern the Company.

The Company's concern only arises when, because of the pattern or amount of drink involved, the employee's attendance, work performance or conduct at work deteriorates.

A breach of these provisions is a disciplinary offence and will be dealt with in accordance with the Company's disciplinary procedure. Depending on the seriousness of the offence, it may amount to gross misconduct and could result in the employee's summary dismissal.

Alcohol and drug related misconduct

Whilst these rules are aimed at assisting employees with alcohol or drug problems, action will nevertheless be taken under the Company's disciplinary procedure if misconduct takes place at work as a result of drinking or taking drugs, or if an employee is found to be under the influence of alcohol or drugs whilst at work. Even a small amount of alcohol can affect work performance and, if an employee is found under the influence of alcohol whilst at work, there could be serious health and safety consequences. The same applies to being under the influence of drugs. Incapacity or misconduct caused by an excess of alcohol or drugs at work is a potential gross misconduct offence under the Company's disciplinary procedure and the employee is therefore liable to be summarily dismissed. This also applies to any employee believed to be buying or selling drugs or in possession of or taking drugs on the Company's premises.

The Company reserves the right in any of these circumstances to arrange for the employee to be escorted from the Company's premises immediately and sent home.

Alcohol and drug testing

On the grounds of health and safety and where necessary to achieve a legitimate business aim, the Company reserves the right to carry out random alcohol and drug screening tests on employees in the workplace. If an employee receives a positive test result, this will be viewed as a potential gross misconduct offence and renders the employee liable to summary dismissal in accordance with the Company's disciplinary procedure. Unreasonable refusal to submit to an alcohol or drug-screening test will also be dealt with through the disciplinary procedure.

CARS AND CAR ALLOWANCES

Company cars

Subject to holding a current, full driving licence, some employees are provided with a car for use in the performance of their job duties. If you are provided with a company car, this will be set out in your contract of employment. Unless you are notified otherwise, a company car may be used for both business and private use, subject to such restrictions and upon such conditions (if any) as the Company may from time to time impose. In particular, the employee is the only person authorised to drive the car. Under no circumstances may any other person drive the car.

Employees are only provided with company cars at the discretion of the Company and it may change its rules and procedures on company cars at any time and from time to time.

The Company reserves the right to set a maximum lease value on company cars and/or to specify the make, model and colour that will be provided.

The Company will pay for the MOT, licensing, insurance, maintenance, repair and servicing of company cars (provided repairs and service are not caused by the employee's negligence or wilful default) and when necessary replacement thereof. However, employees have no contractual right to a replacement car. The Company will also pay for the cost of petrol/diesel (as appropriate) for business use only. The employee must pay for petrol/diesel for all private mileage.

The employee will be responsible for any income tax liability as assessed by the Inland Revenue in respect of the use of the car.

The employee must not permit the car to be taken out of Great Britain without the prior consent of their line manager.

The Company will retain all documents relating to the registration of the car. However, the employee is responsible for ensuring the car has a valid MOT certificate and a valid licence disc and for ensuring the car is properly maintained and serviced. As stated above, the Company will generally bear the cost of these matters.

The employee is also responsible for ensuring the car is properly looked after at all times and is responsible for the cleanliness of it, together with its equipment and fittings. The employee must ensure that it is kept in a roadworthy condition, that it conforms with current road traffic legislation and that the provisions and conditions of the policy of insurance relating thereto are observed and that such policy is not rendered void or voidable. The Company may seek to recoup any losses in the event of damage caused to the car by the employee's negligence or wilful default. In addition, the employee is responsible for the excess which is required to be paid which is not recoverable from the insurance company should the vehicle be involved in an accident, irrespective of the responsibility for the accident. By signing their contract of employment, the employee accepts that the Company shall be entitled to deduct the cost of repair of any such damage and/or the cost of the insurance excess from the employee's wages.

Personal items are left in the car entirely at the employee's own risk and the Company does not accept any liability for loss, theft or damage of personal items.

The employee must report to the Company forthwith:

- vehicle defects

- any road traffic accident in which the employee may be involved whilst driving the car, whether or not that occurred on the Company's business

- any fixed penalty notice or any order of any court to endorse the employee's driving licence or to disqualify him or her from holding a driving licence, whether or not that consequence occurred whilst driving on the Company's business

- any other event which results in the employee being ineligible to drive the car.

The employee is responsible for the payment of any and all fines incurred as a result of a motoring offence whilst the car is in the employee's possession, including parking and speeding fines and by signing their contract of employment the employee accepts that the Company shall be entitled to deduct the cost of any such fines from the employee's wages.

Upon request, the employee must provide his or her full driving licence for inspection.

Failure to observe these rules or failure to use the car in a reasonable and responsible manner may result in the Company withdrawing the use of the car from the employee concerned. In addition, a failure to observe these rules will be regarded as a disciplinary offence and will be dealt with in accordance with the Company's disciplinary procedure. Depending on the seriousness of the breach, it may constitute potential gross misconduct rendering the employee liable to summary dismissal.

In the event that the Company suspends the employee from the performance of his or her duties in accordance with the Company's disciplinary procedure, the employee will not be entitled to the continued use of the car during that period of suspension.

On the termination of the employee's employment, or if he or she ceases to hold a valid and current licence to drive private motor cars, the employee must promptly return or account for the car and deliver up the keys to . . . . *(insert name of contact)*. By signing your contract of employment, you accept that failure to do so will entitle the Company to withhold any outstanding monies/wages due from the Company to you up to the value of the car.

Car allowances

In lieu of the provision of a company car, the employee may elect by notice in writing to the Company to receive a monthly car allowance of such amount as shall be notified by the Company from time to time. This allowance shall be added to and paid on the due date for payment of salary.

Driving and mobile phones

Some employees are required to drive on the Company's business as part of their job duties. Operating a mobile phone whilst driving reduces concentration and increases the likelihood of an accident. It is also now a criminal offence. This section therefore also sets out the Company's requirements in relation to your using a mobile phone whilst driving on Company business. It applies irrespective of whether you use a Company-provided mobile phone or your own personal mobile phone and irrespective of whether you are driving a company car or your own car.

You are completely prohibited from using a hand-held mobile phone or similar hand-held electronic device whilst driving as part of your job duties, whether this is to make or receive telephone calls, send or read text or image/picture messages, send or receive facsimiles or to access the Internet or e-mail. If you are discovered contravening this rule, you will face serious action under the Company's disciplinary procedure. In view of the potential health and safety implications, it may also constitute gross misconduct and could render you liable to summary dismissal. If you do wish to use a hand-held mobile phone when driving, you must stop the car and completely turn off the car's engine before using the mobile phone. A person is regarded as "driving" for the purposes of the law if the engine is running, even if their vehicle is stationary. This means you must not use a hand-held phone at traffic lights, during traffic jams or at other times when the engine is still running.

A hands-free phone is one that does not require you to hold it at any point during the course of its operation. A mobile phone that is attached to fixed speakers and does not require you to hold it whilst in use (for example, because it is stored in a cradle) would be covered, as would a hands-free mobile phone with voice activation. If the phone needs to be held in your hand at some point during its operation, for example to dial the number or to end the call, it is not hands-free. If you are required to drive as part of your job duties and you wish to use your mobile phone, you must ensure you have the appropriate hands-free equipment for the phone. However, even with hands-free equipment, driving and conducting a telephone conversation are both demanding tasks and you should take all reasonable steps to ensure you do not carry out these tasks at the same time. You should therefore make use of any voicemail or call divert facility available, rather than make or receive "live" calls. You should then stop regularly in safe places to check for voicemail messages and to make and return calls. If you do need to make or receive a call whilst driving on Company business and you have the appropriate hands-free equipment, these calls should nevertheless be limited to essential calls and only when it is safe to do so.

CONDUCT WHILST ON COMPANY BUSINESS

As a general rule, what employees do after normal working hours and off Company premises is a personal matter and does not directly concern the Company. However, there are some exceptions to this rule.

The Company will become involved where incidents occur:

- at office parties, office drinks events or other work-related social occasions or gatherings, whether organised by the Company or by employees themselves

- at social occasions or gatherings organised by the Company's customers or clients where the employee has been invited in his capacity as an employee of the Company

- at work-related conferences

- whilst the employee is working away on business on behalf of the Company.

On these occasions, employees are expected to be moderate if drinking alcohol and to behave in an appropriate, mature and responsible manner, taking into account that they are representing the Company. They must take specific action to ensure they are well within the legal limits if they are driving.

Any employee who is found to have harassed or verbally or physically abused or assaulted another employee or a customer or client of the Company, or who otherwise brings the reputation of the Company into disrepute, at such an event will be subject to disciplinary action under the Company's disciplinary procedure. Depending on the circumstances of the case, such behaviour may be treated as gross misconduct and could render the employee liable to summary dismissal.

Where the employee's off-duty conduct seriously undermines the trust and confidence that the Company has in the employee, whether at a work-related social occasion or otherwise, under the Company's disciplinary procedure this could result in the employee's dismissal. For example, if the employee commits a criminal offence outside employment, the Company will examine whether there is an adverse connection between the criminal offence and the employee's employment. The Company will then consider whether the offence is one that makes the employee unsuitable for his type of work or unacceptable to other employees, taking into account length of service, status, relations with fellow workers and the effect on the Company's business and reputation subsequent to a charge or conviction.

Please see the section on Personal Relationships at Work for the Company's policy on employees embarking on a personal relationship with a work colleague.

DATA PROTECTION

In the course of your work you may come into contact with or use confidential information about employees, clients and customers, for example their names and home addresses. The **Data Protection Act 1998** contains principles affecting employees' and other personal records. Information protected by the Act includes not only personal data held on computer but also certain manual records containing personal data, for example employee personnel files that form part of a structured filing system. The purpose of these rules is to ensure you do not breach the Act. If you are in any doubt about what you can or cannot disclose and to whom, do not disclose the personal information until you have sought further advice from .... *(insert name)*, the Company's Data Protection Officer. You should be aware that you can be criminally liable if you knowingly or recklessly disclose personal data in breach of the Act. A serious breach of data protection is also a disciplinary offence and will be dealt with under the Company's disciplinary procedures. If you access another employee's personnel records without authority, this constitutes a gross misconduct offence and could lead to your summary dismissal.

The data protection principles

There are eight data protection principles that are central to the Act. The Company and all its employees must comply with these principles at all times in it's information-handling practices. In brief, the principles say that personal data must be:

1. Processed fairly and lawfully and must not be processed unless certain conditions are met in relation to personal data and additional conditions are met in relation to sensitive personal data. The conditions are either that the employee has given consent to the processing, or the processing is necessary for the various purposes set out in the Act. Sensitive personal data may only be processed with the explicit consent of the employee and consists of information relating to:

   - race or ethnic origin

   - political opinions and trade union membership

   - religious or other beliefs

   - physical or mental health or condition

   - sexual life

   - criminal offences, both committed and alleged.

2. Obtained only for one or more specified and lawful purposes, and not processed in a manner incompatible with those purposes.

3. Adequate, relevant and not excessive. The Company will review personnel files on an annual basis to ensure they do not contain a backlog of out-of-date information and to check there is a sound business reason requiring information to continue to be held.

4. Accurate and kept up-to-date. If your personal information changes, for example you change address, you must inform your line manager as soon as practicable so that the Company's records can be updated. The Company cannot be held responsible for any errors unless you have notified the Company of the relevant change.

5. Not kept for longer than is necessary. The Company will keep personnel files for no longer than six years after termination of employment. Different categories of data will be retained for different time periods, depending on legal, operational and financial requirements. Any data which the Company decides it does not need to hold for a period of time will be destroyed after six months. Data relating to unsuccessful job applicants will only be retained for a period of six months.

6. Processed in accordance with the rights of employees under the Act.

7. Secure, technical and organisational measures will be taken against unauthorised or unlawful processing of personal data and against accidental loss or destruction of, or damage to, data. Personnel files are confidential and are stored in locked filing cabinets. Only authorised staff have access to these files. Files will not be removed from their normal place of storage without good reason. Data stored on diskettes or other removable media will be kept in locked filing cabinets. Data held on computer will be stored confidentially by means of password protection, encryption or coding and again only authorised employees have access to that data. The Company has network back-up procedures to ensure that data on computer cannot be accidentally lost or destroyed.

8. Not transferred to a country or territory outside the European Economic Area unless that country ensures an adequate level of protection for the processing of personal data.

Your consent to personal information being held

The Company holds personal data about you and, by signing your contract of employment, you have consented to that data being processed by the Company. Agreement to the Company processing your personal data is a condition of your employment. The Company also holds limited sensitive personal data about its employees and, by signing your contract of employment, you give your explicit consent to the Company's holding and processing that data, for example sickness absence records, health needs and equal opportunities monitoring data.

Your right to access personal information

You have the right, on request, to receive a copy of the personal information that the Company holds about you, including your personnel file, and to demand that any inaccurate data be corrected or removed. You have the right on request:

- to be told by the Company whether and for what purpose personal data about you is being processed

- to be given a description of the data and the recipients to whom it may be disclosed

- to have communicated in an intelligible form the personal data concerned, and any information available as to the source of the data

- to be informed of the logic involved in computerised decision-making.

Upon request, the Company will provide you with a statement regarding the personal data held about you. This will state all the types of personal data the Company holds and processes about you and the reasons for which they are processed. If you wish to access a copy of any personal data being held about you, you must make a written request for this and the Company reserves the right to charge you a fee of up to £10. To make a request, please complete a Personal Data Subject Access Request Form, which can be obtained from the Data Protection Officer.

If you wish to make a complaint that these rules are not being followed in respect of personal data the Company holds about you, you should raise the matter with the Data Protection Officer. If the matter is not resolved to your satisfaction, it should be raised as a formal grievance under the Company's grievance procedure.

Your obligations in relation to personal information

You should ensure you comply with the following guidelines at all times:

- do not give out confidential personal information except to the data subject. In particular, it should not be given to someone from the same family or to any other unauthorised third party unless the data subject has given their explicit consent to this

- be aware that those seeking information sometimes use deception in order to gain access to it. Always verify the identity of the data subject and the legitimacy of the request, particularly before releasing personal information by telephone

- only transmit personal information between locations by fax or e-mail if a secure network is in place, for example, a confidential fax machine or encryption is used for e-mail

- if you receive a request for personal information about another employee, you should forward this to . . . . *(insert name of contact)* who will be responsible for dealing with such requests

- ensure any personal data you hold is kept securely, either in a locked filing cabinet or, if computerised, it is password protected

- compliance with the Act is your responsibility. If you have any questions or concerns about the interpretation of these rules, take this up with the Data Protection Officer.

DISCLOSURES IN THE PUBLIC INTEREST

The **Public Interest Disclosure Act 1998** protects employees who raise legitimate concerns about specified matters. It makes provision about the kinds of disclosure which may be protected and the circumstances in which disclosures are protected. These rules are therefore intended to comply with the Act by encouraging employees to make disclosures about fraud, misconduct or wrongdoing to the Company, without fear of reprisal, so that problems can be identified, dealt with and resolved quickly.

Qualifying disclosures

Certain kinds of disclosure qualify for protection. These are disclosures of information which are made in good faith and which you reasonably believe tend to show one or more of the following matters is either happening now, took place in the past, or is likely to happen in the future:

- a criminal offence.

- the breach of a legal obligation.

- a miscarriage of justice.

- a danger to the health or safety of any individual.

- damage to the environment.

- deliberate concealment of information tending to show any of the above.

Your belief must be reasonable, but it need not be correct. It might be discovered subsequently that you were, in fact, wrong, but you must be able to show that you held the belief in good faith and that it was a reasonable one to hold in the circumstances at the time. Note that it is not your responsibility to investigate the matter. That is the Company's responsibility.

The disclosure procedure

In order to qualify for protection, there are specified methods of disclosure, or procedures, which you must have followed in order to disclose one of the above matters. The Company encourages you to raise your concerns under this procedure in the first instance. If your concern relates to a breach of your own contract of employment, you should use the Company's grievance procedure. This procedure applies to all employees. In addition, agency workers and contractors who perform functions in relation to the Company are encouraged to use it.

The procedure is as follows:

1. If you wish to make a qualifying disclosure, you should, in the first instance, report the situation to your line manager. If you do not wish to speak to your line manager, you can instead speak to an alternative manager.

2. Such disclosures should be made promptly so that investigation may proceed and any action taken expeditiously.

3. All qualifying disclosures will be treated seriously. The disclosure will be promptly investigated and, as part of the investigatory process, you will be interviewed and asked to provide a written witness statement setting out the nature and details of your qualifying disclosure and the basis for it. Confidentiality will be maintained during the investigatory process to the extent that this is practical and appropriate in the circumstances. However, in order to effectively investigate a disclosure, the Company must be able to determine the scope of the investigation and the individuals who should be informed of or interviewed about the disclosure. The Company reserves the right to arrange for another manager to conduct the investigation other than the manager with whom you raised the matter.

4. The Company will also invite you to attend at least one meeting at a reasonable time and place at which your disclosure can be discussed. You should take all reasonable steps to attend that meeting and you have the right to be accompanied by either a trade union official or a fellow employee of your choice.

5. Once the investigation has been completed and after the meeting with you has taken place, you will be informed in writing of the outcome and the Company's conclusions and decision as soon as possible. You will also be notified in writing of your right to appeal against the Company's decision if you are not satisfied with it. The Company is committed to taking appropriate action with respect to all qualifying disclosures which are upheld.

6. If you wish to appeal against the Company's decision, you must do so in writing within five working days of the Company's decision. On receipt of an appeal, a more senior manager (who may not be the person to whom you addressed your appeal) shall make arrangements to hear your appeal at an appeal meeting. At that meeting you may again, if you wish, be accompanied by either a trade union official or a fellow employee of your choice. You should take all reasonable steps to attend the appeal meeting. Following the meeting, you will be informed in writing of the Company's final decision on your appeal.

7. You will not be penalised for raising a qualifying disclosure even if it is not upheld, unless the complaint was both untrue and made in bad faith.

8. Once the Company's conclusions have been finalised, any necessary action will be taken. This could include either reporting the matter to an appropriate external government department or regulatory agency and/or taking internal disciplinary action against relevant members of staff. If no action is to be taken, the reasons for this will be explained to you.

9. If, on conclusion of the above stages, you reasonably believe that appropriate action has still not been taken, you may then report the matter to the proper authority in good faith. The Act sets out a number of prescribed bodies or persons to which qualifying disclosures may be made. However, the Company always encourages all employees to raise their concerns directly in the first instance, rather than externally. This enables issues to be dealt with promptly and speedily.

General principles

- be aware of the importance of eliminating fraud or wrongdoing at work. Report anything that you become aware of that is illegal

- you will not be victimised, subjected to a detriment or dismissed for raising a legitimate matter under this procedure

- victimisation of an employee for raising a qualifying disclosure under this procedure will be a disciplinary offence and will be dealt with under the Company's disciplinary procedure

- covering up someone else's wrongdoing is also a disciplinary offence. Never agree to remain silent about a wrongdoing, even if told to do so by a person in authority

- finally, maliciously making a false allegation is a disciplinary offence.

DRESS AND APPEARANCE

The Company wishes to portray a professional business image to its clients and customers. As a result, it operates minimum standards of dress and appearance, which require employees to dress in a manner that is suitable and appropriate to the Company's business.

All employees are required to be neat, clean, well-groomed and presentable whilst at work, whether working on the Company's premises or elsewhere on Company business.

If, as part of your job duties, you come into contact with the Company's clients or customers, you must adhere to the following minimum dress and appearance standards:

- you should wear a business suit (comprising jacket plus co-ordinating trousers, skirt or dress) in a discreet colour and a smart shirt or blouse whilst working. Male employees must also wear a tie*

- you should wear smart shoes in a discreet, dark colour*

- hair should be kept neat and well-groomed and hairstyles and hair colours should be conventional*

- jewellery should be kept to a minimum and you should not wear more than one set of earrings. Any earrings worn must be small and unobtrusive*

- nose rings, eyebrow rings and other facial piercings are prohibited*

- tattoos should be kept covered and should not be visible.*

(*Delete as appropriate)

Even if your job does not bring you into contact with the Company's clients or customers, the following are still classed as unacceptable attire for all employees:

- jeans, leggings, combat trousers or torn trousers*

- shorts or miniskirts*

- sports clothing, for example tracksuits and football shirts*

- t-shirts*

- trainers*

- excessive jewellery*.

(*Delete as appropriate)

If your job brings you into contact with machinery, for health and safety reasons your hair must be kept short or tied back at all times and you must not wear jewellery other than a wedding/engagement ring.

Finally, the Company accepts that members of certain ethnic or religious groups are subject to strict religious or cultural requirements in terms of their clothing and appearance. Subject to necessary health and safety requirements, the Company will not insist on dress rules which run counter to the cultural norms of such employees. If you are uncertain as to whether a particular item of clothing is acceptable or not, please speak to . . . . (insert name of contact).

If you fail to comply with the above rules, this is a serious matter and will be dealt with in accordance with the Company's disciplinary procedure. In addition, depending on the circumstances of the case, you may be required to go home and change your clothing. If this happens, you have no right to be paid for the period of your absence from work.

ELECTRONIC AND TELEPHONIC COMMUNICATIONS

Computer misuse

Some employees now have access to computers at work for use in connection with the Company's business. Employees who are discovered unreasonably using the Company's computers for personal and private purposes will be dealt with under the Company's disciplinary procedure.

Vandalism of, or otherwise intentionally interfering with, the Company's computer network constitutes a gross misconduct offence and could render the employee liable to summary dismissal under the Company's disciplinary procedure.

E-mail and the Internet

Some employees also have access to e-mail and the Internet for exclusive use in connection with the Company's business and as part of the normal execution of the employee's job duties. The purpose of these rules is to protect the Company's legal interests. Unregulated access increases the risk of employees inadvertently forming contracts through e-mail and increases the opportunity for wrongful disclosure of confidential information. In addition, carelessly worded e-mail can expose the Company to an action for libel. As such, e-mail to clients and customers must follow the Company's designated house style, which will be supplied to authorised users. Failure to follow house style is a disciplinary matter and will be dealt with under the Company's disciplinary procedure. E-mail should not be used for unsolicited correspondence or marketing campaigns and employees may not commit the Company financially by e-mail unless they have been granted a specific level of delegated authority to do so.

Employees who are authorised users are not permitted to surf the Internet or to spend excessive time "chatting" by e-mail for personal and private purposes during their normal working hours. Employees are also prohibited from using e-mail to circulate any non-business material. Not only does excessive time spent online lead to loss of productivity and constitute an unauthorised use of the Company's time, sexist, racist or other offensive remarks or jokes sent by e-mail are capable of amounting to unlawful harassment. Employees who are discovered contravening these rules may face serious disciplinary action under the Company's disciplinary procedure. Depending on the seriousness of the offence, it may amount to gross misconduct and could result in the employee's summary dismissal. Use of instant messaging systems must be expressly approved in advance by the Company.

Logging on to sexually explicit websites or the downloading and/or circulation of pornography or obscene material or using the Internet for gambling or illegal activities constitutes gross misconduct and could render the employee liable to summary dismissal under the Company's disciplinary procedure.

The Company reserves the right to monitor employees' e-mails and use of the Internet, both during routine audits of the computer system and in specific cases where a problem relating to excessive or unauthorised use is suspected. The purposes for such monitoring are:

- to promote productivity and efficiency

- for security reasons

- to ensure there is no unauthorised use of the Company's time e.g. that an employee has not been using e-mail to send or receive an excessive number of personal communications

- to ensure the smooth running of the business if the employee is absent for any reason and communications need to be checked

- to ensure that all employees are treated with respect, by discovering and eliminating any material that is capable of amounting to unlawful harassment.

Communications of a sensitive or confidential nature should not be sent by e-mail because it is not guaranteed to be private. When monitoring e-mails, the Company will, save in exceptional circumstances, confine itself to looking at the address and heading of the e-mails. However, where circumstances warrant it, the Company may open e-mails and access the content. In this case, the Company will avoid, if possible, opening e-mails clearly marked as private or personal.

The Company reserves the right to deny or remove e-mail or Internet access to or from any employee.

Computer software, games and viruses

The Company licences the use of computer software from a variety of outside companies. The Company does not own this software and, unless authorised by the software developer, neither the Company nor any of its employees have the right to reproduce it. To do so constitutes an infringement of copyright. Contravention is a disciplinary matter and will be dealt with in accordance with the Company's disciplinary procedure.

The Company's computer network makes it vulnerable to viruses. Therefore, only duly authorised personnel have the authority to load new software onto the network system. Even then, software may be loaded only after having been checked for viruses by authorised personnel. Any employee found to be contravening this will face disciplinary action under the Company's disciplinary procedure.

Employees may only access any computer games that are on the network outside their normal working hours.

Telephone misuse

The Company's telephone lines are for the exclusive use by employees in connection with the Company's business. Whilst the Company will tolerate essential personal telephone calls concerning an employee's domestic arrangements, excessive use of the telephone for personal calls is prohibited. This includes lengthy, casual chats and calls at premium rates.

Not only does excessive time engaged on personal telephone calls lead to loss of productivity, it also constitutes an unauthorised use of the Company's time. If the Company discovers that the telephone has been used excessively for personal calls, this will be dealt with under the Company's disciplinary procedure and the employee will be required to pay to the Company the cost of personal calls made.

Acceptable telephone use should be no more than . . . . *(insert a suitable figure)* minutes of personal calls in each working day. Personal telephone calls should be timed so as to cause minimum disruption to the employee's work and should, as a general rule, only be made during breaks except in the case of a genuine emergency.

Employees should be aware that telephone calls made and received on the Company's telephone network will routinely be monitored and recorded to assess employee performance, to ensure customer satisfaction and to check that the use of the telephone system is not being abused. If employees wish to make or take a particularly sensitive, private or confidential personal telephone call, they are advised that they can use the following telephone: . . . . *(insert details)* which will not be subject to any form of monitoring or recording by the Company.

EQUAL OPPORTUNITIES AND DIGNITY AT WORK

Policy statement

The Company is an equal opportunity employer and is fully committed to a policy of treating all its employees and job applicants equally.

The Company will take all reasonable steps to employ, train and promote employees on the basis of their experience, abilities and qualifications without regard to race, colour, ethnic origin, nationality, national origin, religion or belief, sex, sexual orientation, marital status, age or disability. The Company will also take all reasonable steps to provide a work environment in which all employees are treated with respect and dignity and that is free of harassment based upon an employee's race, colour, ethnic origin, nationality, national origin, religion or belief, sex, sexual orientation, marital status, age or disability. The Company will not condone any form of harassment, whether engaged in by employees or by outside third parties who do business with the Company.

Employees have a duty to co-operate with the Company to ensure that this policy is effective in ensuring equal opportunities and in preventing discrimination or harassment. Action will be taken under the Company's disciplinary procedure against any employee who is found to have committed an act of improper or unlawful discrimination, harassment, bullying or intimidation. Serious breaches of this equal opportunities and dignity at work statement will be treated as potential gross misconduct and could render the employee liable to summary dismissal. Employees should also bear in mind that they can be held personally liable as well as, or instead of, the Company for any act of unlawful discrimination.

Employees should draw the attention of their line manager to suspected discriminatory acts or practices or suspected cases of harassment. Employees must not victimise or retaliate against an employee who has made allegations or complaints of discrimination or harassment or who has provided information about such discrimination or harassment. Such behaviour will be treated as potential gross misconduct in accordance with the Company's disciplinary procedure.

Recruitment, advertising and selection

The recruitment process will be conducted in such a way as to result in the selection of the most suitable person for the job in terms of experience, abilities and qualifications. The Company is committed to applying its equal opportunities policy statement at all stages of recruitment and selection.

Advertisements will encourage applications from all suitably qualified and experienced people. When advertising job vacancies, in order to attract applications from all sections of the community, the Company will, as far as reasonably practicable:

1. Ensure advertisements are not confined to those publications which would exclude or disproportionately reduce the numbers of applicants of a particular gender, sexual orientation, religion or racial group.

2. Avoid prescribing any unnecessary requirements which would exclude a higher proportion of a particular gender, sexual orientation, religion or racial group or which would exclude disabled job applicants.

3. Avoid prescribing any requirements as to marital status.

4. Where vacancies may be filled by promotion or transfer, they will be published to all eligible employees in such a way that they do not restrict applications from employees of any particular gender, sexual orientation, religion or racial group or from employees with a disability.

5. Ensure that the setting of age limits as a criterion of any specific job is justifiable.

The selection process will be carried out consistently for all jobs at all levels. All applications will be processed in the same way. The staff responsible for short-listing, interviewing and selecting candidates will be clearly informed of the selection criteria and of the need for their consistent application. Wherever possible, all applicants will be interviewed by at least two interviewers and all questions asked of the applicants will relate to the requirements of the job. The selection of new staff will be based on the job requirements and the individual's suitability and ability to do, or to train for, the job in question.

With disabled job applicants, the Company will have regard to its duty to make reasonable adjustments to work arrangements or to work premises in order to ensure that the disabled person is not placed at a substantial disadvantage in comparison with persons who are not disabled.

Training and promotion

The Company will train all line managers in the Company's policy on equal opportunities and in helping them identify discriminatory acts or practices or acts of harassment or bullying. Line managers will be responsible for ensure they actively promote equal opportunity within the departments for which they are responsible.

The Company will also provide training to all employees to help them understand their rights and responsibilities in relation to dignity at work and what they can do to create a work environment free of bullying and harassment.

Where a promotional system is in operation, it will not be discriminatory and it will be checked from time to time to assess how it is working in practice. When a group of workers predominantly of one race, religion, sex or sexual orientation or a worker with a disability appears to be excluded from access to promotion and training and to other benefits, the promotional system will be reviewed to ensure there is no unlawful discrimination.

Terms of employment, benefits, facilities and services

All terms of employment, benefits, facilities and service will be reviewed from time to time, in order to ensure that there is no unlawful discrimination on the grounds of race, colour, ethnic origin, nationality, national origin, religion or belief, sex, sexual orientation, marital status, age or disability.

Equal pay

The Company is committed to equal pay in employment. It believes its male and female employees should receive equal pay for like work, work rated as equivalent or work of equal value. In order to achieve this, the Company will endeavour to maintain a pay system that is transparent, free from bias and based on objective criteria.

Harassment

It is against the Company's policy for any employee, male or female, to sexually harass another employee or to harass him or her on the grounds of actual or perceived sexual orientation. It is also against the Company's policy for any employee to harass another employee on the grounds of his or her race, colour, ethnic origin, nationality, national origin, religion or belief, age or disability. Harassment occurs where a person engages in unwanted conduct which has the purpose or effect of violating the other's dignity at work or creating an intimidating, hostile, degrading, humiliating or offensive work environment for the other person.

Sexual harassment includes, but is not limited to, unwelcome sexual advances, requests for sexual favours, engaging in other unwelcome verbal or physical conduct of a sexual nature, subjection to obscene or other suggestive comments, and sexual jokes or pictures. Racial harassment includes, but is not limited to, engaging in unwelcome verbal or physical conduct of a racial nature, subjection to racist comments, and racist jokes or pictures. Harassment may comprise intentional bullying which is obvious or violent but it can also be unintentional or subtle, such as the use of nicknames or teasing. It is for the complainant to decide for him or herself what they regard as offensive.

Reporting complaints

All allegations of discrimination or harassment will be dealt with seriously, confidentially and speedily. The Company will not ignore or treat lightly grievances or complaints of discrimination or harassment from members of a particular sex, sexual orientation, religion or racial group or from employees who are disabled.

With cases of harassment, while the Company encourages employees who believe they are being harassed to notify the offender (by words or by conduct) that his or her behaviour is unwelcome, the Company also recognises that actual or perceived power and status disparities may make such confrontation impractical.

If you wish to make a complaint of discrimination or harassment, you should follow the following steps:

1. First of all, report the incident of discrimination or harassment to your line manager. If you do not wish to speak to your line manager, you can instead speak to an alternative manager or to a member of the personnel department.

2. Such reports should be made promptly so that investigation may proceed and any action taken expeditiously.

3. All allegations of harassment will be taken seriously. The allegation will be promptly investigated and, as part of the investigatory process, you will be interviewed and asked to provide a written witness statement setting out the nature and details of the incident or complaint and the basis for it. Confidentiality will be maintained during the investigatory process to the extent that this is practical and appropriate in the circumstances. However, in order to effectively investigate an allegation, the Company must be able to determine the scope of the investigation and the individuals who should be informed of or interviewed about the allegation. The Company reserves the right to arrange for another manager to conduct the investigation other than the manager with whom you raised the matter.

4. The Company will also invite you to attend at least one meeting at a reasonable time and place at which your complaint can be discussed. You should take all reasonable steps to attend that meeting and you have the right to be accompanied by either a trade union official or a fellow employee of your choice.

5. Once the investigation has been completed and after the meeting with you has taken place, you will be informed in writing of the outcome and the Company's conclusions and decision as soon as possible. You will also be notified in writing of your right to appeal against the Company's decision if you are not satisfied with it. The Company is committed to taking appropriate action with respect to all complaints of discrimination or harassment that are upheld.

6. If you wish to appeal against the Company's decision, you must do so in writing within five working days of the Company's decision. On receipt of an appeal, a more senior manager (who may not be the person to whom you addressed your appeal) shall make arrangements to hear your appeal at an appeal meeting. At that meeting you may again, if you wish, be accompanied by either a trade union official or a fellow employee of your choice. You should take all reasonable steps to attend the appeal meeting. Following the meeting, you will be informed in writing of the Company's final decision on your appeal.

7. You will not be penalised for raising a complaint of discrimination or harassment even if it is not upheld, unless the complaint was both untrue and made in bad faith.

Any employee who is found to have discriminated against or harassed another employee in violation of this policy will be subject to disciplinary action under the Company's disciplinary procedure. Such behaviour may be treated as gross misconduct and could render the employee liable to summary dismissal. In addition, line managers who had knowledge that such discrimination or harassment had occurred in their departments but who had taken no action to eliminate it will also be subject to disciplinary action under the Company's disciplinary procedure.

Monitoring equal opportunity and dignity at work

The Company will regularly monitor the effects of selection decisions and personnel and pay practices and procedures in order to assess whether equal opportunity and dignity at work are being achieved. This will also involve considering any possible indirectly discriminatory effects of its working practices.

FLEXIBLE WORKING

It is the Company's view that the promotion of flexible working arrangements increases staff motivation, performance and productivity, reduces stress and encourages staff retention by enabling employees to balance their work life with their other priorities.

The statutory right

Employees who are parents of young or disabled children have a statutory right to apply for a change to the terms and conditions of their employment to have flexible working arrangements to look after their children. In order to make a request under the statutory right, you must have worked for the Company for a continuous period of six months at the date of application. You must also meet *each* of the following eligibility criteria:

- you have responsibility for the upbringing of either a child under six or a disabled child under 18

- you are either the mother, father, adopter, guardian or foster parent of the child or you are married to or the partner of the child's mother, father, adopter, guardian or foster parent

- you are making the request to help care for the child

- you are making the request no later than two weeks before the child's sixth birthday or 18th birthday where the child is disabled

- you have worked continuously for the Company for the previous 26 weeks

- you have not made a request to work flexibly under the statutory right during the past twelve months.

Flexible working generally

In addition to statutory rights, it is the Company's policy to try and be flexible on working patterns for all employees, although priority will always be given to those employees who do have the statutory right to request flexible working so that the Company can comply with its legal obligations. You may therefore wish to apply for flexible working to accommodate charity work, leisure activities, other caring arrangements or external study. All employees are eligible to apply for flexible working regardless of their seniority, current working pattern, age, sex, race, religion, sexual orientation, whether they have a disability or whether they are employed on a permanent or fixed-term basis.

You can apply to vary the number of hours you work, the times you work or your place of work (between your home and the Company's place of business). Although the Company is committed to being flexible on working patterns for its employees, you must recognise that the requirements of the business are paramount and it may not be appropriate or possible for flexible working arrangements to apply to all jobs across all areas of the business.

The flexible working application procedure

You should comply with the following procedure to make your application for flexible working arrangements:

- make your request in writing setting out the flexible working arrangement you seek. A Flexible Working Application Form can be obtained from . . . . *(insert name of contact)*

- within 28 days of receipt of your application, the Company will set up a meeting with you to discuss the changes you have proposed, the effect of the proposed changes and any possible alternative work patterns that might suit. You may be accompanied at this meeting

- the Company will consider your request and will make a practical business assessment on whether, and if so, how it could be accommodated

- the Company will notify its decision to you within 14 days of the meeting. If the Company accepts your request, it will write to you, establishing a start date and providing a written note of the contract of employment variation. If your application is refused, the Company will explain the grounds for refusal in writing and confirm the internal appeal procedure

- where your request is agreed to, it constitutes a permanent change to your terms and conditions of employment. This means you do not have the right to revert to your previous pattern of working at a future date

- you can appeal in writing against a refusal within 14 days of receipt of the Company's rejection letter. The Company will then set up a meeting with you to discuss your appeal within 14 days after receiving your appeal letter. After that meeting has been held, the Company will write to you within 14 days to notify you of the outcome of your appeal.

Grounds for refusal

The Company may refuse your flexible working application on one or more of the following grounds:

- the burden of additional costs

- the detrimental effect it would have on the Company's ability to meet customer demand

- the Company's inability to reorganise work amongst existing staff

- the Company's inability to recruit additional staff

- the detrimental impact it would have on quality

- the detrimental impact it would have on performance

- the insufficiency of work available during the period when you proposed to work

- the Company's planned structural changes.

In refusing an application, the Company will provide details relating to why the particular ground applies in the circumstances.

Please note that each request for flexible working will be dealt with individually, taking into account the likely effects the changes will have on the Company, the work of the department in which you are employed, your work colleagues and the particular circumstances of the case. This means that if the Company agrees to one employee's request, this does not set a precedent or create a right for another employee to be granted the same or a similar change to their work pattern.

GIFTS FROM CLIENTS/SUPPLIERS

The Company's aim is always to ensure customer and client satisfaction. Occasionally, satisfied customers, clients or other third parties may seek to reward employees with gifts. Whilst the Company has no desire to stop deserving employees receiving a reward from a satisfied customer or client, there is the potential for the abuse of a client's or customer's generosity. In addition, certain suppliers offer "reward schemes" which allow employees to obtain free gifts in return for ordering services or products from that supplier. The Company needs to be sure its suppliers are competitive and that its employees are acting in the best interests of the Company. As such, the Company needs to ensure that there is a culture of honesty and transparency in the practice of receiving gifts, whether from customers, clients or suppliers. For these purposes a "gift" is any payment or item given to an employee on an apparently ex-gratia basis by any party who is the Company's actual or potential client, customer or supplier.

If you receive a gift, you must report this to your line manager as soon as it is given to you. If you fail to do so, this constitutes a disciplinary offence and will be dealt with in accordance with the Company's disciplinary procedure. If an employee in a clear position of trust fails to report the receipt of a gift, this may be treated as gross misconduct in accordance with the Company's disciplinary procedure and could render the employee liable to summary dismissal.

If the Company discovers that a supplier has been used by an employee wholly or mainly because of the incentive of a free gift (and, as such, the employee has not acted in the best interests of the Company), this will also constitute a disciplinary offence and will be dealt with under the Company's disciplinary procedure. Depending on the seriousness of the offence, it may again be treated as gross misconduct and could render the employee liable to summary dismissal.

Unless the giver of the gift specifically states the gift is intended for a particular employee as a personal reward, all gifts are deemed to belong to the Company. Whether you will be permitted to keep the gift in these circumstances is at the Company's absolute discretion.

HEALTH AND SAFETY

The Company is committed to ensuring the health, safety and welfare of its employees, and it will, so far as is reasonably practicable, establish procedures and systems necessary to implement this commitment and to comply with its statutory obligations on health and safety. It is the responsibility of each employee to familiarise themselves and comply with the Company's procedures and systems on health and safety.

While the Company will take all reasonable steps to ensure the health and safety of its employees, health and safety at work is also the responsibility of the employees themselves. It is the duty of each employee to take reasonable care of their own and other people's health, safety and welfare and to report any situation which may pose a serious or imminent threat to the well being of themselves or of any other person. If an employee is unsure how to perform a certain task or feels it would be dangerous to perform a specific job or use specific equipment, then it is the employee's duty to report this as soon as possible to their line manager, their health and safety representative or the safety officer. Alternatively, an employee may, if they prefer, invoke the Company's formal grievance procedure or they may make a complaint under the Company's provisions on Disclosures in the Public Interest.

Disciplinary action under the Company's disciplinary procedure may be taken against any employee who violates health and safety rules and procedures or who fails to perform their duties under health and safety legislation. Depending on the seriousness of the offence, it may amount to potential gross misconduct rendering the employee liable to summary dismissal.

The Company will provide and maintain a healthy and safe working environment with the objective of minimising the number of instances of occupational accidents and illnesses. The Company will pay particular attention to:

1. Maintaining the workplace in a safe condition and providing adequate facilities and arrangements for welfare at work.

2. Providing a safe means of access to and egress from the workplace.

3. The provision and maintenance of equipment and systems of work that are safe.

4. Arrangements for ensuring safety to health in connection with the use, handling, storage and transport of articles and substances.

5. The provision of such information, instructions, training and supervision as is necessary to ensure the health and safety at work of its employees and other persons.

The Company also recognises its duty to protect the health and safety of all visitors to the Company, including contractors and temporary workers, as well as any members of the public who might be affected by the Company's work operations.

Organisation

The Board of the Company has overall responsibility for health and safety in the Company. . . . . *(insert name of contact)* is the safety officer and has responsibility for overseeing, implementing and monitoring health and safety procedures in the Company and for reporting back to the Board on health and safety matters. The safety officer also conducts regular inspections of the workplace, maintains safety records and investigates and reports on accidents at work.

In addition, a number of employees have been delegated as health and safety representatives. Further details can be obtained from . . . . *(insert name of contact)*.

Training

Safety training is an integral part of an effective health and safety programme. It is essential that every employee is trained to perform their job safely. All employees will be trained in safe working practices and procedures. Training will include instruction on the safe use of any equipment provided.

Employees at special risk

The Company recognises that some workers may from time to time be at increased risk of injury or ill-health resulting from work activities. The Company therefore requires that all employees advise their line manager if they become aware of any change in their personal circumstances which could result in their being at increased risk. This could include medical conditions, permanent or temporary disability, taking medication and pregnancy.

First aid and reporting accidents at work

First aid boxes are located at strategic points around the workplace. All employees will be shown the location of the nearest first aid box and will be given the names of the designated first aid personnel. This information is also displayed on works notice boards.

All injuries, however small, sustained by a person at work must be reported to their line manager or the safety officer and recorded in the accident book. Accident records are crucial to the effective monitoring of health and safety procedures and must therefore be accurate and comprehensive. The safety officer will inspect the accident book on a regular basis and all accidents will be investigated and a report prepared, with any necessary action being taken to prevent a recurrence of the problem.

Fire

Fire is a significant risk within the workplace. All employees have a duty to conduct their operations in such a way as to minimise the risk of fire and they are under a duty to report immediately any fire, smoke or potential fire hazards, such as faulty electric cable or loose connections. Employees should never attempt to repair or interfere with electrical equipment or wiring themselves. The safety officer is responsible for the maintenance and testing of fire alarms and fire fighting, prevention and detection equipment.

Smoke detectors and manually operated fire alarms are located at strategic points throughout the workplace. If a smoke detector sounds or fire is discovered, it is the responsibility of any employee present to activate the alarm and evacuate the building. Fire extinguishers are also located at strategic points throughout the workplace. Employees are expected to tackle a fire themselves only if it would pose no threat to their personal safety to do so. If the situation is dangerous or potentially dangerous, the employee should activate the fire alarm and evacuate the building immediately.

Fire doors designed to slow the spread of fire and smoke throughout the workplace have been installed at strategic points. Fire doors are designed to close automatically after opening and must never be blocked or wedged open. Fire exits are also located at strategic points throughout the workplace. Fire exit doors and corridors must never be locked, blocked or used as storage space. All employees must ensure they are familiar with their evacuation route and designated assembly point in case of fire. Practice fire drills will be conducted on a regular basis to ensure employee familiarity with emergency evacuation procedures.

Emergency lighting has been installed in exit corridors and above emergency exit doors in case of power failure. Lifts also have emergency lighting installed although they should not be used in the case of an emergency evacuation.

Company safety rules

- all employees should be aware of and adhere to the Company's rules and procedures on health and safety

- all employees must immediately report any unsafe working practices or conditions to their line manager, their health and safety representative or to the safety officer

- horseplay, practical joking, running in the workplace, misuse of equipment or any other acts which might jeopardise the health and safety of any other person are forbidden

- any person whose levels of alertness are reduced due to illness or fatigue will not be allowed to work if this might jeopardise the health and safety of any person

- employees must not adjust, move or otherwise tamper with any electrical equipment or machinery in a manner not within the scope of their job duties

- all waste materials must be disposed of carefully in the receptacles provided and in such a way that they do not constitute a hazard to other workers

- no employee should undertake a job which appears to be unsafe

- no employee should undertake a job until they have received adequate safety instruction and they are authorised to carry out the task

- all injuries must be reported to the employee's line manager or to the safety officer

- all materials must be properly and safely used and when not in use properly and safely secured

- work should be well-planned to avoid injuries in the handling of heavy materials and while using equipment

- employees should take care to ensure that all protective guards and other safety devices are properly fitted and in good working order and must immediately report any defects to their line manager or to the safety officer

- suitable clothing and footwear must be worn at all times. Personal protective equipment must be worn where appropriate

- work stations and work sites must be kept clean and tidy and any spillage must be cleaned up immediately

- employees should use handrails when going up and down stairs, should never read while walking, must close filing cabinet drawers when not in use and must keep all floor areas free of obstruction.

Access

- walkways and passageways must be kept clear and free from obstructions at all times

- if a walkway or passageway becomes wet it should be clearly marked with warning signs and any liquid spilt on the floor should be wiped up immediately

- trailing cables should not be left in any passageway

- where objects are stored in or around a passageway, care must be taken to ensure that no long or sharp edges jut out into the passageway

- where a passageway is being used by vehicles or other moving machinery, an alternative route should be used by pedestrians where possible. If no alternative route is available, the area must be clearly marked with warning signs.

Tools and equipment

- company machinery, tools and equipment are only to be used by qualified and authorised personnel

- it is the responsibility of all employees to ensure that any tools or equipment they use are in a good and safe condition. Any tools or equipment which are defective must be reported to a line manager or to the safety officer

- all tools must be properly and safely stored when not in use

- no tool should be used without the manufacturer's recommended shields, guards or attachments

- approved personal protective equipment must be properly used where appropriate

- persons using machine tools must not wear clothing, jewellery or long hair in such a way as might pose a risk to their own or anyone else's safety

- employees are prohibited from using any tool or piece of equipment for any purpose other than its intended purpose.

Manual handling

- lifting and moving of objects should always be done by mechanical devices rather than manual handling wherever reasonably practicable. The equipment used should be appropriate for the task at hand

- the load to be lifted or moved must be inspected for sharp edges and wet patches

- when lifting or moving a load with sharp or splintered edges, gloves must be worn

- the route over which the load is to be lifted should be inspected to ensure it is free of obstructions

- employees should not attempt to lift or move a load which is too heavy to manage comfortably. Employees should ask for assistance if there is any danger of strain

- when lifting an object off the ground, employees should assume a squatting position, keeping the back straight. The load should be lifted by straightening the knees, not the back

- employees should not attempt to obtain items from shelves which are beyond their reach. A ladder or stepping stool should be used. Employees should not use chairs or any makeshift device for climbing and should never climb up the shelves themselves.

HOLIDAYS

Your paid annual leave entitlement is set out in your contract of employment.

The Company's holiday year runs from . . . . *(insert date)* to . . . . *(insert date)*. You must use all of your holiday entitlement by the last day of each holiday year and, unless there are exceptional circumstances and unless approved in writing in advance by your line manager, you may not carry your holiday entitlement forward into the next holiday year. Holiday entitlement not used by the correct date will usually be lost and under no circumstances will payment in lieu be made for holiday entitlement that is lost through not being exercised by the correct date.

All requests for annual leave must be approved in writing in advance by your line manager. You must not book holidays until your request has been formally authorised. You should endeavour to give as much notice as possible of proposed annual leave dates. In any event, such notice must be at least twice the number of days' leave as that you wish to take as annual leave. The Company will try to co-operate with your holiday plans where possible, but this is always subject to the requirements of the Company's business and to adequate staffing levels being maintained at all times.

No more than two weeks' paid annual leave may be taken at any one time without the prior written agreement of your line manager.

In your first and last year of employment, your holiday entitlement will be that proportion of your annual holiday entitlement equivalent to the proportion of the holiday year in question during which you have been employed. This will be calculated to the nearest half day and assuming that holiday entitlement accrues at an even rate from day to day. During your first year of service, unless otherwise agreed in writing by your line manager, you will not normally be permitted to take more annual leave than you have actually accrued at the time the holiday is taken. Entitlement during your first year of service is calculated monthly in advance at the rate of one-twelfth of the full year's entitlement.

Should you be incapacitated for work due to sickness or injury during any period of pre-booked annual leave (whether in whole or in part) the Company may in its absolute discretion reimburse the period of annual leave entitlement lost due to incapacity. You have no contractual right to reimbursement and, before considering whether reimbursement is appropriate in the circumstances, you must deliver to the Company a relevant medical certificate covering the period of incapacity. Reimbursement will only be considered where you fell seriously ill or you sustained a serious injury.

On the termination of your employment, you are entitled to be paid for any accrued annual leave for that holiday year that has not been taken by the date of termination.

If, on the date of termination of your employment, you have taken more annual leave than you have accrued in that holiday year, you will be required to reimburse the Company in respect of such unearned annual leave. The Company shall be entitled, as a result of your agreement to the terms of your contract of employment, to deduct the value of the unearned annual leave from any final payment of salary to be made to you.

No payment in lieu of accrued contractual annual leave will be made to you in the event of the termination of your employment for gross misconduct or in the event that you give inadequate notice to terminate your employment or you leave before your contractual notice period has expired. In addition, contractual annual leave will not accrue during a period of additional maternity leave or during a period of sickness absence, except at the absolute discretion of the Company. For these purposes, contractual annual leave means any leave entitlement provided for in your contract of employment that is over and above the four-week statutory annual leave entitlement provided for in the **Working Time Regulations 1998**.

LEAVES OF ABSENCE

Paid annual leave

The provisions relating to your entitlement to paid annual leave are set out in your contract of employment and in the section on Holidays.

Religious holidays

Subject to complying with the relevant provisions as to notice set out in your contract of employment and to the requirements of the Company's business, you will normally be allowed to use your annual leave entitlement to observe special religious holidays.

Jury service and other public duties

Should you be called up for jury service or required to attend court to give evidence as a witness, you must notify your line manager as soon as reasonably practicable. Time off work will normally be granted in these circumstances. You will be required to provide a copy of the court summons to support your request for time off work.

You have no contractual or statutory right to be paid for time not worked due to jury service or other related public duties. Any payment of salary by the Company during this period is done so in its absolute discretion and will be subject to the deduction of any monies received from the court in respect of loss of earnings. You must therefore submit a claim to the court for loss of earnings and claim the full allowance available to you.

If on any day on which you attend court you are told that your services are not required, you must then return to work and report to your line manager before starting work.

Membership of the reserved armed forces

If you are a member of the reserved armed forces, you may use your paid annual leave entitlement to carry out your duties, provided you comply with the provisions relating to paid annual leave set out in your contract of employment and in the section on "Holidays". The Company expects you to use your paid annual leave first before applying for further time off.

Otherwise, any further time off relating to membership of the reserved armed forces will only be granted at the absolute discretion of the Company and you have no contractual or statutory right to be paid for this leave. Any payment of salary made by the Company in such circumstances is done so in its absolute discretion. If you wish to apply for this type of leave, you should apply in writing to . . . . *(insert name of contact)* stating the period of leave requested and the reasons for it.

Medical appointments

Appointments with doctors, dentists and other medical practitioners should, as far as reasonably practicable, be made outside of your normal hours of work or with the minimum disruption to the working day (i.e. made at the beginning or end of the working day).

Time off work to attend medical appointments must be authorised by your line manager in advance. In any event, unless there are exceptional circumstances, no more than two hours should be taken off work for any one appointment. You have no contractual or statutory right to be paid for absences relating to attendance at medical appointments. Any payment of salary during attendance at such appointments is made at the absolute discretion of the Company.

Compassionate leave

Subject to your statutory right to time off to deal with a family emergency (see the section on Time Off for Dependants), if you suffer a bereavement or serious illness in your family or in a close relationship, compassionate leave must be approved by your line manager. All requests for compassionate leave will be considered on an individual basis.

There is no contractual or statutory entitlement to be paid for absences relating to compassionate leave. Any payment of salary during compassionate leave is made at the absolute discretion of the Company.

Subject to your statutory right to time off to deal with a family emergency, the Company expects you to use your paid annual leave entitlement for time off needed to care for sick relatives or friends.

Special unpaid leave

The Company may, in certain circumstances, consider requests for special unpaid leave, for example, for the purposes of education, family responsibilities or for important personal reasons. However, the Company expects you to use your paid annual leave first. Otherwise, any further time off for special reasons will only be granted at the absolute discretion of the Company and you have no contractual or statutory right to be paid for this leave. If you wish to apply for special leave, you should do so in writing to . . . . *(insert name of contact)* stating the period of leave requested and the reasons for it. Requests for special leave will be assessed on their individual merits and circumstances. Special leave is operated entirely at the discretion of the Company and it may be withdrawn at any time.

General

Failure to return from leave and report for work on the due date of return without reasonable excuse is a disciplinary offence and will be dealt with in accordance with the Company's disciplinary procedure.

MATERNITY

The Company implements the maternity rights set out in legislation. The maternity rules are complex and so if you become pregnant you should clarify the relevant procedures with .... *(insert name of contact)* to ensure you follow them correctly. It is also important that, as an expectant mother, you keep your line manager updated regarding your intentions in relation to antenatal care and work (i.e. both when leaving to begin your maternity leave and when planning to return to work). The Company encourages open discussion between you and your line manager to ensure that questions and problems about maternity rights can be discussed and resolved as quickly as possible.

The following abbreviations are used in this section:

EWC   Expected Week of Childbirth - the week in which your baby is likely to be born. Sunday is the beginning of the week.

SMP   Statutory Maternity Pay.

QW   The Qualifying Week for SMP - the 15th week before the EWC.

On becoming pregnant, you should notify your line manager as soon as you feel able to do so. In addition, you will need to provide a MATB1 certificate. The MATB1 is issued by your doctor or midwife and it states when your baby is due. It must have either your doctor's name and address on it or, if issued by a midwife, her name and registration number.

Maternity rights

You have the following key maternity rights:

- time off for antenatal care

- maternity pay - linked to your level of earnings and your length of service

- maternity leave - the period of leave is dependent on your length of service.

Time off for antenatal care

During pregnancy, you are allowed time off work with pay to attend the antenatal clinic and other antenatal appointments made on the advice of your doctor or midwife. Antenatal care may include relaxation and parent craft classes, as well as medical examinations. Except in the case of your first appointment, an appointment card must be produced to your line manager. You must endeavour to give your line manager as much advance notice as possible of antenatal appointments and you should try to arrange them as close to the start or the end of your working day as possible.

Statutory maternity pay

To be eligible to receive SMP, you must have been employed by the Company for at least 26 weeks ending with the QW. In addition, your average weekly earnings in the eight weeks up to and including the QW must have been at least equal to the lower earnings limit for National Insurance contributions. To take advantage of the right to SMP, you must also give the Company proper notification (see further below).

SMP is paid for up to 26 weeks after commencement of your maternity leave. It is paid into your bank account in the same way as salary is normally paid and it is subject to deductions of income tax and National Insurance contributions. There are two rates of SMP, known as the higher rate and lower rate. The higher rate of SMP is paid for the first six weeks. It is equivalent to 90% of your average weekly earnings. For the purpose of calculating average weekly earnings, shift allowance (if applicable), on-call allowance, over-time and commission are included. The lower rate of SMP is paid for the remaining 20 weeks and is £102.80 per week or a rate equivalent to 90% of your average weekly earnings if this is less than £102.80 per week. Payment of SMP cannot begin until the Sunday after you leave work to start your maternity leave.

SMP is payable only for weeks in which you do no work for the Company. If you decide to return to work before the end of your SMP entitlement, you will not be paid SMP for the weeks worked. Instead, you will receive your normal salary. SMP is payable whether or not you intend to return to work for the Company after your maternity leave.

The maternity pay period can begin at any time from the start of the eleventh week before the EWC. However, if you decide to work up to when your baby is born, the maternity pay period will start from the Sunday following the date of birth.

It is important for maternity pay purposes that you notify your line manager if, during the maternity pay period, you are either taken into legal custody or you start to work for another employer.

If you have been working for the Company for less than 26 weeks at the QW or you do not have the necessary level of earnings, you are not eligible to receive SMP. You may, however, be able to apply to the Department for Work and Pensions for Maternity Allowance if you meet their qualifying conditions.

Maternity leave

There are two categories of maternity leave:

* ordinary maternity leave

* additional maternity leave.

The amount of time allowed for maternity leave is linked to your length of service with the Company.

Ordinary maternity leave

All pregnant employees are entitled to 26 weeks' ordinary maternity leave. This applies regardless of the length of your service or the number of hours you work. Your contract of employment continues during ordinary maternity leave and you are entitled to receive all your contractual benefits, except for salary. This means, for example, that holiday entitlement will continue to accrue. This also includes other benefits such as: pension contributions, private medical insurance, life assurance and permanent health insurance. On resuming work after ordinary maternity leave, you will be entitled to benefit from any general pay increases that may have been awarded in your absence.

Even if you do not want to take 26 weeks off work, the law requires all employees to take a minimum of two weeks of maternity leave immediately after the birth of the child. This is known as the compulsory maternity leave period.

You should endeavour to take any outstanding annual leave that may be due to you before the commencement of your ordinary maternity leave and you are reminded that annual leave must be taken in the holiday year in which it is earned: see the section on Holidays for further information.

Additional maternity leave

If you have completed 26 weeks' continuous service with the Company by the fifteenth week before your EWC, you will be entitled to take additional maternity leave. Additional maternity leave starts immediately after the end of your ordinary maternity leave and continues for a further 26 weeks. Your contract of employment continues during additional maternity leave but only some terms of the contract will continue. The terms and conditions which apply during additional maternity leave are:

- are entitled to benefit from the Company's implied obligation of trust and confidence

- you are bound by your implied obligation to the Company of good faith

- you are entitled to receive your contractual notice period if your employment is terminated

- you must give the Company the notice provided for in your contract if you wish to terminate your employment

- the terms and conditions in your contract of employment relating to disciplinary and grievance procedures will continue to apply

- you are bound by the terms in your contract relating to disclosure of confidential information and participation in any other business.

During your additional maternity leave, entitlement to statutory annual leave under the **Working Time Regulations 1998** will continue to accrue, but all further contractual annual leave entitlement (including entitlement to paid bank holidays) will cease. Contractual annual leave accrual will recommence when you return to work after additional maternity leave.

Commencing maternity leave: notice requirements

You are required to notify the Company in writing of your intention to take maternity leave by the 15th week before the EWC. You must notify the Company:

- that you are pregnant

- when your EWC will be

- when you intend your maternity leave and SMP to start.

You are permitted to change your mind about when you want to start your maternity leave providing you give the Company at least 28 days' written notice of the revised start date.

Once you have notified your maternity leave plans, the Company will write to you within 28 days, setting out the date on which we expect you to return to work if you take your full entitlement to maternity leave.

Note that maternity leave may commence no earlier that the eleventh week before the EWC. The latest it may begin is the date of birth itself. If you give birth before the date you have notified, then your maternity leave begins automatically on the date of the birth. You must notify the Company as soon as is reasonably practicable of the date of birth.

Returning to work after maternity leave: notice requirements

If you intend to return to work before the end of your ordinary or additional maternity leave, you must give the Company at least 28 days' notice of your date of return. If you fail to do so, we may postpone your return to such a date as will give the Company 28 days' notice, provided that this is not later than the end of your maternity leave period.

You are not legally obliged to give advance notice to the Company if you intend to return to work immediately after the end of your ordinary or additional maternity leave. You may simply return on your due day of return. That said, if you qualify for additional maternity leave and you want to return after the end of ordinary maternity leave, you must still give us 28 days' notice. If you fail to give the appropriate notice, we may postpone your return to such a date as will give the Company 28 days' notice, provided that this is not later than the end of your additional maternity leave.

If you unable to attend work at the end of your ordinary or additional maternity leave due to sickness or injury, the Company's normal arrangements for sickness absence will apply.

If you do not intend to return to work at all after your maternity leave, you are still required to give the Company written notice of the termination of your employment as set out in your contract of employment.

Your rights on return to work

On resuming work after ordinary maternity leave, you are entitled to return to the same job on the same terms and conditions as if you had not been absent. On resuming work after additional maternity leave, again you are entitled to return to the same job on the same terms and conditions as if you had not been absent. If, however, there is some reason why it is not reasonably practicable for the Company to take you back in your original job, you will be offered suitable alternative work of equivalent status and responsibility.

If you are a full-time employee, you have no automatic right to return to work on a part-time basis at the end of your maternity leave. Likewise, you have no automatic right to work from home. However, all requests for part-time or home work will be considered in line with the operational requirements of the Company. It is the Company's policy to promote flexible working arrangements for all employees and in particular for women returning from maternity leave. Further details, including the procedure to be followed, can be found in the section on Flexible Working. If you would like this option to be considered, please speak to your line manager as far in advance of your return as possible in order that the relevant procedure can be put into operation.

Pregnancy-related illnesses

If you are absent from work due to a pregnancy-related illness after the beginning of the fourth week before the EWC but before the date you have notified, or before you have notified a date, on which you intend to commence your maternity leave, then your maternity leave will begin automatically on the first day of your absence. You must notify the Company that you are absent from work wholly or partly because of pregnancy as soon as is reasonably practicable and, until your maternity leave commences, you are still required to comply with the reporting procedure set out in the section on Sickness Absence.

PARENTAL LEAVE

The Company implements the parental leave rights set out in legislation. Parental leave is additional to paternity leave, maternity leave and time off to deal with family emergencies (see the sections on Paternity Leave, Maternity and Time Off for Dependants). Both mothers and fathers can take parental leave. Parental leave is unpaid.

In order to qualify for parental leave, you must have worked for the Company (or, to the extent that this is permitted by the regulations, for a previous employer) for a continuous period of one year by the time you want to take the leave.

You are entitled to take up to 13 weeks' parental leave in order to care for a natural or an adopted child (or to make arrangements for the child's welfare) if you meet one of the following eligibility conditions:

- you are the natural parent of or you have acquired formal parental responsibility for a child who is under five years old

- you have adopted a child under the age of 18

- you are the parent of a child who was under the age of five on December15, 1999 or a child placed with you for adoption in the five years ending on that date (provided in this case you take your parental leave by March 31, 2005 at the latest).

If you are the parent or adoptive parent of a disabled child who has been awarded Disability Living Allowance, you are entitled to take up to 18 weeks' parental leave.

Assuming you are eligible, you can choose to take parental leave:

- up until the child's fifth birthday

- in adoption cases, for five years after the child is first placed with you for adoption (or until the child's 18th birthday if that comes sooner)

- in the case of a child with a disability, up until the child's 18th birthday.

Parental leave is for each child, so in the case of twins, 13 weeks' leave may be taken for each child. You must take parental leave in blocks of one week. The exception to this is that parents of disabled children can take leave in blocks of one day. A maximum of four weeks' parental leave can be taken in respect of any child during any one calendar year.

You are required to give at least 21 days' written notice to your line manager of your proposed parental leave. If leave is to be taken immediately after birth or adoption, 21 days' written notice of the expected week of childbirth or the expected week of placement for adoption should be given. You must specify the dates on which your period of parental leave is to start and finish. A Parental Leave Request Form can be obtained from . . . . (insert name of contact).

The Company reserves the right to postpone a period of parental leave for up to six months where it considers the operation of its business would be unduly disrupted if the leave were to be taken at the time requested. For example, leave may be postponed during particularly busy periods, seasonal peaks or where a significant proportion of your department have already applied to be absent from work at the same time. The Company will confirm any postponement arrangements in writing no later than seven days after receipt of your notice to take parental leave. This letter will state the reason for postponement and set out the new dates of parental leave. The Company will not postpone leave if you have given notice to take it immediately after the time the child is born or is placed with you for adoption.

You will be required to produce evidence to confirm you are the parent or the person who is legally responsible for the child. This will take the form of production of a copy of the child's birth certificate or the adoption papers and/or a copy of the letter awarding Disability Living Allowance for a disabled child. For new employees, the Company reserves the right to make enquiries of previous employers to find out how much parental leave has already been taken.

At the end of parental leave, you will be entitled to return to the same job provided always that your period of parental leave was for a period of four weeks or less.

There is no contractual or statutory entitlement to be paid for absences relating to parental leave. Any payment of salary during parental leave is made at the absolute discretion of the Company.

Finally, if you act dishonestly in claiming an entitlement to parental leave, this is a disciplinary offence and will be dealt with under the Company's disciplinary procedure. Depending on the seriousness of the offence, it may amount to potential gross misconduct and could result in your summary dismissal.

PATERNITY LEAVE

The Company implements the paternity leave rights set out in legislation. Paternity leave is additional to both parental leave and time off to deal with family emergencies (see the sections on Parental Leave and Time Off for Dependants). It is also additional to paid annual leave entitlement.

In order to qualify for the right to take paternity leave, you must have worked for the Company for a continuous period of 26 weeks by the week that falls 15 weeks before the week in which the child is expected to be born. In respect of an adopted child, the period is calculated as at the week in which the child's adopter is notified of having been matched with the child for adoption. You must also meet each of the following eligibility criteria:

- you have, or expect to have, responsibility for the upbringing of the child

- you are either the biological father or adopter of the child or you are married to or the cohabiting partner of the child's mother or adopter

- you are making the request to help care for the child or support the child's mother.

Assuming you are eligible, you are able to take up to two weeks' paid paternity leave. You can take this in a single block of either one or two weeks. Odd days cannot be taken. Paternity leave can start either from the date the child is born or from a chosen number of days or weeks after the date of childbirth (or, in respect of an adopted child, from the date of placing for adoption). It can start on any day of the week, but it must be completed within eight weeks of the date of childbirth (or date of placement for adoption). If the child is born early, it must be completed within the period from the date of childbirth up to eight weeks after the expected date of childbirth.

In the case of multiple births, for example, twins, note that only one period of paternity leave is available.

During paternity leave, most employees will be entitled to statutory paternity pay. The rate of statutory paternity pay is £102.80 per week or a rate equivalent to 90% of your average weekly earnings if this is less than £102.80 per week. Employees who earn less than the lower earnings limit for National Insurance purposes are not eligible to receive statutory paternity pay.

If you wish to request to take paternity leave, you must inform your line manager in writing of your request no later than the 15th week before the expected week of childbirth. You must provide written details of when the child is due, whether you wish to take one or two weeks' paternity leave and when you want your paternity leave to start. A Paternity Leave Request Form can be obtained from . . . . *(insert name of contact).*

In the case of an adopted child, you must give written notice of your intention to take paternity leave no later than seven days after the date on which notification of the match with the child is given by the adoption agency. The notice must specify the date on which the adopter was notified of having been matched with the child, the date the child is expected to be placed for adoption, whether you wish to take one or two weeks' paternity leave and when you want your paternity leave to start.

You are able to change your mind about the date on which you want your paternity leave to start provided you give at least 28 days' written notice of the new date to your line manager.

PERSONAL RELATIONSHIPS AT WORK

The Company recognises that employees who work together may form personal friendships and, in some cases, close personal relationships. The Company does not, as a general rule, wish to interfere with such personal friendships and relationships. However, it must also ensure that employees continue to behave in an appropriate, professional and responsible manner at work and that they continue to fulfil their job duties both diligently and effectively. These rules are therefore aimed at striking a balance between your right to a private life and the Company's right to protect its business interests.

The following rules apply to employees embarking on close personal relationships at work, whether the relationship is with a fellow worker, client, customer, supplier or contractor:

- you must not allow your relationship to influence your conduct at work. Intimate behaviour during normal working hours or on Company or client premises is prohibited. This includes holding hands, other close physical contact, discussions of a sexual nature or kissing

- if you embark on a relationship with another employee in your department, you should declare this to your line manager as soon as reasonably practicable

- if you are a manager and you embark on a relationship with a more junior member of staff, you should declare this to a Director as soon as reasonably practicable. This is particularly important if you are the line manager of the employee because of the risk of the junior employee being afforded more favourable treatment, or less favourable treatment if the relationship subsequently breaks down. In order to avoid a situation where you have managerial authority over a junior member of staff with whom you are having a relationship, the Company reserves the right to elect to transfer one or both of you to a job in another department, either on a temporary basis or permanently. The Company will first consult with both of you to try and reach an amicable agreement on transfer

- if you begin a relationship with a client, customer, supplier or contractor and allows the potential for you to abuse your level of authority, you must declare the relationship to your line manager or a Director as soon as reasonably practicable. In these circumstances, the Company reserves the right to elect to transfer you to a job in another department where you will not be able to exert undue influence over the other party, either on a temporary basis or permanently. The Company will first consult with you to try and reach an amicable agreement on transfer

- if a personal relationship (or the breakdown of a personal relationship) starts to affect your performance or conduct at work, then your line manager will speak to you with a view to your previous level of performance or conduct being restored. However, if your performance or conduct fails to improve or it reverts to a problem level, the matter will become a disciplinary one

- if you are having or have had a personal relationship and you are found to have afforded either more or less favourable treatment to the other employee because of this relationship or you have exercised undue influence over a client, customer, supplier or contractor, this is a disciplinary matter.

A breach of these rules is a disciplinary offence and will be dealt with under the Company's disciplinary procedure. Depending on the seriousness of the offence, it may amount to gross misconduct and could result in your summary dismissal.

PROVISION OF ACCOMMODATION

Some employees may be provided with residential accommodation for the better performance of their job duties. If you are provided with accommodation to enable you to properly carry out your duties, this will be set out in your contract of employment. Your contract of employment will also state whether the accommodation provided is furnished or unfurnished and whether it is for occupation by you alone or whether your spouse or partner and children are also able to reside there.

Any accommodation provided by the Company will be for as long as the employee remains in the Company's employment and will be provided entirely for the better performance of the employee's job duties. The employee will occupy the premises as a service licensee only and that right to occupy the premises will cease immediately on the termination of the employee's employment for whatever reason, with the notice period provided for in the employee's contract of employment. On the expiry of the contractual notice period, the employee must then vacate the premises forthwith.

During employment, the employee will be required to reside at the premises and must keep the interior of the premises clean, tidy and in good decorative repair. Noise must be kept to an acceptable level at all times. The employee must immediately notify the Company of any damage to the premises or its fixtures and fittings and to any furnishings provided. The Company may seek to recoup any losses in the event of damage caused to the premises or its fixtures, fittings or furnishings by the employee's negligence or wilful default. By signing their contract of employment, the employee accepts that the Company shall be entitled to deduct the cost of repair of any such damage or the cost of replacement of the damaged item (as appropriate) from the employee's wages.

The employee is not permitted to assign, sublet or part with possession of the premises or, other than as set out in their contract of employment, to have anyone live with them at the premises or stay overnight as a guest without the prior written consent of the Company.

Any breach of these provisions will be dealt with under the Company's disciplinary procedure and, depending on the circumstances of the case, it could amount to potential gross misconduct rendering the employee liable to summary dismissal. This will result in the employee being required to vacate the premises with immediate effect.

The Company [will/will not] be responsible for any gas, electricity, telephone, water, council tax, television licensing, contents insurance or other related charges.

The Company shall have the unrestricted right to enter the premises without notice at any time and from time to time and for any reason as it considers fit.

The Company's provision of residential accommodation to an employee does not under any circumstances give rise to a service tenancy.

REDUNDANCY

Should circumstances arise where redundancy may be a possibility because fewer employees are needed to perform the Company's work, the first steps the Company will take will be to:

- reduce overtime to a workable minimum

- restrict recruitment

- investigate measures such as short-time working and/or lay-offs

- investigate whether there are opportunities for redeployment to other departments within the Company

- explore other methods by which desired cost cuts could be achieved

- explore whether there are any other options available in order to avoid redundancy.

If redundancies cannot be avoided, the Company will give consideration to terminating agency workers and asking for volunteers. Whilst the Company will aim to keep the number of compulsory redundancies to a minimum, the overriding consideration will always be the future needs of the business.

If the need for compulsory redundancies arises, the selection of employees for redundancy will be in accordance with the section on Selection Criteria and there will be full consultation with employees throughout the redundancy selection process. Employees will be notified at the earliest possible opportunity of the reasons for the potential redundancy situation and of the Company's proposals.

REIMBURSEMENT OF EXPENSES

Expenses incurred by employees will be reimbursed in accordance with these rules. These rules are designed to provide for the reimbursement of reasonable out-of-pocket expenses wholly, exclusively, necessarily and actually incurred by an employee engaged on the business of the Company.

In order to claim back expenses, you must complete and sign a claim form, have it countersigned by your line manager and then submit it to . . . . *(insert name of contact)*. You are expected to provide original VAT receipts for expenditure incurred where this is reasonably practicable and you should give a full description of the expenditure incurred and why it was necessary. You should ensure all expense claims are made and submitted promptly.

The Company does not advance expenses.

Travelling expenses

The Company will reimburse travelling expenses necessarily incurred for business purposes. This is generally limited to the cost of travel from the Company's office to the business destination and return. Journeys between an employee's home and normal place of work are considered private and do not constitute business travel. Under no circumstances should you claim the cost of your journeys from home to your normal place of work.

The following expenses will be paid:

- where you use your own car, mileage allowance at a rate per mile as determined by the Company from time to time and notified to you. In this case, ensure you record your actual mileage undertaken. Your car must be comprehensively insured for use while on Company business

- where you have a Company car, the cost of fuel you have used in connection with Company business

- standard class rail or coach fares

- taxi fares where suitable public transport is not available

- economy class air fares (provided your line manager has authorised this in advance).

The Company is not responsible for any fines or penalty fares which you may receive while on Company business. The responsibility for paying such fines or penalties is yours.

Subsistence expenses

If you are required to stay away from home overnight on Company business, you may claim the costs of overnight accommodation (i.e. evening dinner, bed and breakfast only) at an appropriate hotel or guest house approved in advance by your line manager. The Company will not reimburse items of a personal nature such as alcoholic drinks, newspapers and private telephone calls.

If you are required to leave the office on Company business for more than . . . . *(insert number)* hours but you are not staying away overnight, day subsistence will be payable at rates determined by the Company from time to time and notified to you.

Telephone calls

The cost of telephone calls made using your private telephone or mobile phone, in connection with Company business, will be reimbursed. Itemised telephone bills are required to support this expense claim.

Staff and client entertainment

Only line managers are permitted to claim back expenses incurred for staff entertaining.

Client entertaining means hospitality provided by the Company or its employees to non-Company employees in connection with the business of the Company. You must judge what is reasonable in the circumstances and it should normally be possible for your line manager to agree to a level of entertaining expenditure before the commitments are made.

Other expenses

You should seek the prior approval of your line manager before incurring other expenses.

RESIGNATION

Should you decide to leave the Company, written notice of your resignation must be given to your line manager. The amount of notice you are required to give to terminate your employment is set out in your contract of employment.

An early leaving date may be mutually agreed, at the absolute discretion of your line manager, and subject to the requirements of the Company's business.

A copy of your resignation letter will be forwarded to . . . . *(insert name of contact)*, who will formally acknowledge it, confirm your last day of employment and provide details of the final salary payments due to you. They will also ask you to complete an exit questionnaire and/or attend an exit interview (see below).

It is both unfortunate and expensive when an employee decides to leave the Company. It is important that the Company finds out the reason why to avoid losing staff in the future. Once an employee has resigned, they are more likely to give an honest input, which is invaluable to the Company. Therefore, if you decide to leave the Company, you will be approached by . . . . *(insert name of contact)* who will ask you to attend an exit interview and/or complete an exit questionnaire. This interview/questionnaire represents an ideal opportunity for the Company to gather information about why you decided to leave. With your permission, selected information gained from the interview and/or from your completed questionnaire will be discussed with your line manager. The aim of this is to ensure that any problem issues can be discussed and resolved before you leave.

Finally, on your last day of work it will be necessary for you to return to your line manager any items of Company property which are in your possession, such as clothing, equipment, keys, swipe card, etc.

RIGHT TO SEARCH

Whilst most employees are loyal and trustworthy, it is an unfortunate fact that some employees may occasionally be dishonest or they may try to bring drugs or alcohol into the workplace in contravention of the Company's rules and procedures (see the section on Alcohol and Drugs).

In order to counter these potential problems, the Company reserves the right to carry out personal searches of employees in the workplace. Searches will be conducted having regard to the section on Equal Opportunities and Dignity at Work and entirely on a random basis. They may be carried out at any time whilst an employee is in the workplace.

Searches will be confined to requesting the employee to empty out the contents of their pockets or bag and to remove any jackets, coats, shoes or other outer clothing. Employees will be searched by either a line manager or a designated security officer who is of the same sex as the employee being searched and the search will take place in private. If the employee to be searched would like to have a fellow employee present to act as a witness, this will be arranged.

The Company will keep a record of all personal searches conducted, including the date, time and results of each search and the identities of the employee and the searching officer. This information will be stored confidentially. It will be reviewed on a regular basis by . . . . *(insert name of contact)* to ensure that searches are being carried out fairly and randomly.

If you refuse to submit to a personal search without reasonable excuse, this is a serious matter and will be dealt with in accordance with the Company's disciplinary procedure.

SICKNESS ABSENCE

Should you be unable to attend work due to illness or injury, you must comply with the following sickness absence reporting procedure:

1. On the first morning of your sickness absence, you must contact the Company and speak to your line manager at the earliest possible opportunity and as close to your normal start time as possible. In any event, this must be no later than two hours after your normal start time. If you are unable to speak to your line manager personally, you should speak to . . . . *(insert name of contact).* You should give details of the nature of your illness and, if the illness is of a minor nature, you should indicate when you believe you will be fit to return to work. You must inform your line manager as soon as possible of any change in the date of your anticipated return to work.

2. For an absence of seven consecutive calendar days or less, you are required to telephone your line manager on a daily basis in accordance with the reporting procedure set out above. You must also complete a self-certification of sickness absence form immediately on your return to work. Self-certification forms are available from (and should be returned once completed to) . . . . *(insert name of contact).* You are reminded that it is a serious disciplinary offence to provide false information on a self-certification form.

3. Should your sickness absence be for a period in excess of seven calendar days, you are required as an absolute minimum to contact your line manager on a weekly basis in order to provide an update on your illness or injury. A doctor's certificate must also be obtained. A new doctor's certificate must be submitted each week. Your doctor's certificate must be forwarded to . . . . *(insert name of contact)* as quickly as possible and in any event no later than the end of the calendar week in respect of which the certificate applies.

4. You should have certificates (either self-certification of sickness absence forms or doctor's certificates) to cover the entire period of your sickness absence.

5. For all periods of sickness absence of half a day or longer, your line manager may require you to attend a "back to work" interview on your return to work to discuss the reasons for your absence and, in particular, whether it was work-related.

6. For long-term sickness absence, your line manager may request to visit you at home.

7. For long-term sickness absence or frequent periods of sickness absence, the Company may request a medical report from your GP or consultant or alternatively request that you visit a doctor selected by the Company to undergo a medical examination. The cost of any such report or examination will be met by the Company and you are required to co-operate in the obtaining and disclosure of all results and reports to the Company. The Company will only request you to undergo a medical examination where reasonable to do so.

8. The Company reserves the right to withhold sick pay in circumstances where the certification procedure described above has not been followed or where there is sufficient reason to doubt the validity of your sickness absence claim. In the latter circumstances, the Company may request you to undergo a medical examination by a doctor selected by it.

9. On being fit to return to work, you must contact your line manager and let them know as far in advance as possible of the proposed date of your return.

Persistent short-term sickness absence is, in the absence of any underlying medical condition or other reasonable excuse, a disciplinary matter and will be dealt with in accordance with the Company's disciplinary procedure.

SMOKING

In order to enable employees to work in a smoke-free environment, the Company's business premises are designated "no smoking". Smoking is prohibited in all areas of the Company's premises at all times, including the area immediately outside the entrance to the premises [except the area which has been specifically designated as a smoking area. The following room has been designated as a smoking area: .... *(insert details)*. The smoking area must be kept fire safe at all times].

The Company's prohibition on smoking applies not only to employees but also to visitors to the workplace, including clients and customers.

If you wish to smoke, you must do this in your own time either outside your normal hours of work or during your lunch break. You are not permitted to take additional smoking breaks during the day.

Failure to comply with the above rules is a disciplinary offence and will be dealt with in accordance with the Company's disciplinary procedure. Where the smoking creates a clear health and safety hazard, then such behaviour constitutes potential gross misconduct and could render the employee liable to summary dismissal.

STRESS AT WORK

The Company recognises that its employees are its most important asset and it is committed to providing the support and assistance necessary to enable its employees to undertake their job duties in an environment that is as stress-free as possible. The Company's aim is to ensure employees' health and safety at work and that they are not subjected to excessive workloads, onerous working practices or a detrimental work environment. Employees who have high stress levels are more likely to work inefficiently, behave erratically, have low morale and be absent from work. Work performance will then suffer.

The Company is committed to providing a support system to help minimise and alleviate stress in the workplace. It is the Company's intention to deal constructively and sympathetically with stress. Stress will not be treated as a sign of weakness. If you feel that your work performance or your health is suffering because of stress-related matters, whether those matters are occurring outside the workplace or within the work environment, you should first raise this with your line manager. Your line manager will arrange a meeting with you to discuss the matter with a view to taking the appropriate steps to remove the cause of the stress or to assist you to deal with it. This may include evaluating the amount and complexity of your workload, your work environment and/or referring the matter to a more senior manager who may be in a better position to provide guidance and to take the appropriate steps to assist. Alternatively, if your stress is in your view entirely work-related, you may if you prefer invoke the Company's formal grievance procedure or you may make a complaint under the Company's provisions on Equal Opportunities and Dignity at Work.

The Company also provides professional stress counselling with independent, trained counsellors through an advice helpline (telephone number: . . . . *(insert telephone number))*. This is an entirely confidential service and any discussions an employee has with a stress counsellor will be strictly confidential unless the employee agrees otherwise. All employees are encouraged to make use of this service if they are feeling stressed for whatever reason. They will be able to obtain advice concerning their condition, the causes of it and appropriate action which might be taken to assist them. Employees are also free to seek help themselves from their own doctor or counsellor. However, please note that if you do not tell the Company you are suffering from stress and unable to cope or if the Company is unaware that you have a particular problem or vulnerability, we will not be in a position to help you.

Finally, the Company has carried out a stress audit on all aspects of its business to ensure that, so far as reasonably practicable, it does not expose any employees to unnecessarily high stress levels in its work practices and work environment. This audit will be reviewed on a periodic basis.

TIMEKEEPING

All employees are expected to report for work punctually and to observe the normal hours of work laid down in their contract of employment. Failure to report for work on time is detrimental to the efficient running of the business and imposes an unnecessary burden on colleagues.

If you are going to be late for work, you must make every effort to contact your line manager by telephone as soon as reasonably practicable to notify them of this fact and of the time you expect to arrive. If you are then late for work, you must report to your line manager and explain the reason for your lateness before starting work.

If it becomes necessary for you to leave work before your normal finishing time or to take time off work during normal working hours (even in circumstances of a family emergency), prior authorisation must be obtained from your line manager. You must then report to your line manager on re-starting work. In respect of family emergencies, please see the section on Time Off for Dependants for further information.

Except in the normal course of your job duties and during your lunch break, you must not leave your place of work without prior authorisation from your line manager.

Your line manager will monitor your timekeeping on an ongoing basis. Such monitoring will include visual observation and/or electronic swipe-card data (where appropriate).

You have no contractual or statutory right to be paid for time not worked due to lateness or absence. Any payments made by the Company in such circumstances are done so in its absolute discretion.

Failure to comply with the above rules and procedures without reasonable excuse and/or persistent poor timekeeping are serious offences and will be dealt with in accordance with the Company's disciplinary procedure.

TIME OFF FOR DEPENDANTS

All employees are entitled to take a reasonable amount of time off during normal hours of work in order to deal with family emergencies. You have no contractual or statutory right to be paid for absences relating to family emergencies. Any payment of salary during time off is made at the absolute discretion of the Company.

The right to take time off enables you to deal with an unexpected or sudden problem and make any necessary longer term arrangements:

- if a dependant falls ill or has been involved in an accident or assaulted

- when your partner is having a baby

- to make longer-term care arrangements for a dependant who is ill or injured

- to deal with the death of a dependant, for example, making funeral arrangements

- to deal with an unexpected disruption or breakdown in care arrangements for a dependant, for example, when a childminder fails to turn up

- to deal with an incident involving your child whilst they are at school.

For these purposes, a "dependant" is your spouse, partner, child or parent or someone who lives with you as part of your family. It does not include tenants, boarders or employees living in your family home. In cases of illness, injury or where care arrangements break down, a dependant may also be someone who reasonably relies on you for assistance. This may be where you are the primary carer or the only person who can help in an emergency.

In the event of a family emergency occurring while you are at work, you must immediately inform your line manager of the nature of the emergency and seek their express permission to leave work early.

In the event of a family emergency occurring outside your normal hours of work which will prevent you from reporting to work at your normal start time, you must contact the Company and speak to your line manager at the earliest possible opportunity and as close to the normal start time as possible. In any event, this must be no later than two hours after your normal start time. If you are unable to speak to your line manager personally, you should speak to . . . . *(insert name of contact)*. You should give details of the nature of the emergency, the reason for your absence and how long you expect to be absent from work. Where the emergency is ongoing, you must report to your line manager on a daily basis and always at least one hour before your normal start time. You must update your line manager on the reason for the ongoing absence and how long you expect it to continue. You must inform your line manager as soon as possible of any change in the date of your anticipated return to work.

The Company envisages that the amount of leave taken will, in most cases, be one or two days at most. The leave to which you are entitled is enough to help you cope with the immediate crisis. You must actively seek alternative longer-term care arrangements for the care of a dependant within one day of the emergency occurring. Should it not be possible to make such arrangements, you must contact your line manager and explain why further absence is required. Authorisation of such continued absence will be at the absolute discretion of your line manager. The right to time off under these rules is intended to cover unforeseen family emergencies. If you know in advance that you are going to need time off, then you should speak to your line manager about the possibility of taking such time as part of your annual leave entitlement.

The Company reserves the right to ask you to provide supporting evidence of the family emergency on your return to work. You must also complete a Family Emergencies Absence Form immediately on your return. These forms are available from . . . . (insert name of contact). You are reminded that it is a serious disciplinary offence to knowingly provide false information on a Family Emergencies Absence Form or to dishonestly claim a right to time off to deal with a family emergency. Any offence will be dealt with in accordance with the Company's disciplinary procedure and, depending on the circumstances, could amount to gross misconduct rendering you liable to summary dismissal.

In the event of a dispute between you and your line manager about whether a particular incident or occurrence falls under the terms of these rules, a Director shall be responsible for determining whether the request for time off made by you relates to a genuine family emergency. Their decision shall be final.

USE OF COMPANY EQUIPMENT

In order to enable certain employees to work from home or otherwise away from the Company's premises, the Company may provide them with designated items of office equipment. Office equipment may include a computer, laptop, printer, scanner, telephone, fax machine, answer machine, mobile phone, desk, chair, filing cabinet or any other item of office equipment. If you are provided with any items of office equipment, you will be responsible for ensuring they are properly looked after, stored and otherwise kept safely at all times. You will be required to pay to the Company the replacement cost of any item of office equipment which is lost or stolen whilst under your control due to your negligence or deliberate or reckless act or omission.

The Company reserves the right to require you to return any item of office equipment at any time during your employment for any reason whatsoever, including, but not limited to, the withdrawal of the privilege of working from home and/or working away from the Company's premises. You have no contractual entitlement to the use of the office equipment and therefore withdrawal of its use at any time does not entitle you to claim damages or compensation. In addition, on the termination of your employment for any reason, you must promptly and without unreasonable delay return any items of office equipment and, in any event, this must take place no later than any date specified to you at the time by the Company. Any items of office equipment must be returned in the same condition as provided to you, subject to reasonable wear and tear. If an item of office equipment is damaged whilst under your control, reasonable wear and tear excepted, you are required to pay to the Company the cost of repairing the damage. In certain circumstances, this may include the replacement cost of the office equipment if it cannot, in the Company's reasonable opinion, be repaired.

Any office equipment is provided for the exclusive use by you in connection with your employment with the Company. Use of the office equipment for personal and private purposes is prohibited. If you are discovered using the equipment for personal or private purposes, this is a disciplinary matter and will be dealt with under the Company's disciplinary procedure. A deliberate, negligent or reckless failure to take proper care of an item of office equipment, resulting in it being lost, damaged or stolen, is also a disciplinary offence and will again be dealt with in accordance with the Company's disciplinary procedure.

If you are to be allocated one or more items of office equipment for use at your home or away from the Company's premises, you will be asked to sign a form acknowledging receipt of the equipment. By signing this form, you also provide your written consent for the Company to deduct a sum equal to the market value of any item of office equipment (or the cost of repair) from your wages, as defined in s.27 of the **Employment Rights Act 1996**, should it be lost, stolen or damaged whilst under your control due to your negligence or deliberate or reckless act or omission or should you fail to return it to the Company either when demanded or in the event of the termination of your employment.

Section IV

Disciplinary and
grievance procedures

Disciplinary and grievance procedures

Dealing with conduct and other disciplinary matters is one of the most difficult challenges for any employer. Make a wrong move and an employee can exact a high price. And even if you've a good reason to take action, tribunals demand that you follow the right procedure to the letter. This section shows you how to play it safe and stay on the right side of the law.

WHY IT MATTERS?

You only have to open the papers to read of another tribunal claim involving an allegedly wronged worker. And if it's in the press it'll come with a big headline - normally associated with a huge compensation award. OK, so the reality is that most awards don't reach five figures or attract the media. Point is, there's a growing trend amongst some workforces to "have a go". You can hardly blame them - over the past decade a stack of new employment laws have been introduced and as you'd expect they're not slanted in your favour. However, you can't run away from disciplinary issues - if you ignore them you'll create an even greater problem. In this section we've included the key documents you need to help stay on the straight and narrow. It's all about covering your back with the right paperwork and following the correct procedures.

FORMAL OR INFORMAL?

Before you can even think about some kind of sanction, naturally, you need a good reason, e.g. misconduct. Be sure of your evidence before you confront the employee - getting your facts straight is vital, so a detailed investigation will be necessary. Then, you need to decide whether to tackle the matter through informal counselling or whether to opt for the formal disciplinary route. Cases of minor misconduct or unsatisfactory performance are usually best dealt with informally through informal counselling or coaching. There will, however, be situations where matters are more serious or where an informal

approach has not worked. If informal action does not bring about an improvement, or the situation is considered to be too serious to be classed as minor, consider taking formal disciplinary action.

HEAR WHAT?

The first step in the formal procedure will be to arrange a disciplinary hearing. Use our *Notification of Disciplinary Hearing* letter to get things off on the right footing. It explains what the employee's rights are, how he should prepare for it and what the format will be. It also complies with the new statutory dismissal and disciplinary procedure. Once you've had the hearing you need to think about whether a warning is appropriate - don't issue a pre-typed warning there and then. This looks like you've pre-judged the issue. Instead, at least sleep on your decision. If a written warning or final written warning is deemed appropriate it's vital that you cover all the bases. Use the sample warning letters we've included. First warnings are normally valid for six months and final warnings for up to twelve months. After a disciplinary hearing has taken place, you may actually decide that no formal action is appropriate. In this case, use the *Confirmation of No Further Disciplinary Action* letter.

OUT THE DOOR

If you followed the warnings procedure to its natural conclusion, it means that a dismissal is inevitable, but only after a disciplinary hearing. Again, it's vital that the dismissal letter dots all the Is and crosses all the Ts - to help reduce the chance of any comeback. Our *Dismissal with Notice Letter* for misconduct will serve as a prompt to ensure everything's covered, e.g. what's the situation in respect of accrued holiday pay?

NOT QUITE!

Once you've made your decision that's the end of the matter right? Not quite. It's essential that you allow the employee the right of appeal against any decision reached in the disciplinary procedure. This is because you're required to follow the so-called rules of natural justice, as well as complying with the statutory dismissal and disciplinary procedure. This means someone other than you should consider the facts to see if the decision reached was fair. Use the *Notice of Disciplinary Appeal Hearing* letter to explain the procedure to the employee and point out his rights. After the appeal hearing, confirm the outcome using the *Letter Following Disciplinary Appeal Hearing*.

NOT A BAD BOY, BUT...

What if the employee's not misbehaving but just isn't pulling his weight - his work's not up to scratch? Then you need to address performance issues via first, a **Notice of Performance Review Meeting** and then, a **Warning of Poor Performance** letter. The emphasis of this letter is very much on support, e.g. the offer of additional training. However, it also makes plain that if the employee fails to accept your offers, he's in danger of being dismissed (ultimately).

BELIEF SUSPENDED

What if there's an allegation of serious misconduct but you need the employee off your premises so that you can carry out a full investigation? Then use the **Suspension Letter**. This letter indicates that suspension is a neutral act, not indicating guilt. Normally the period should be paid - so keep it to an absolute minimum. If after a disciplinary hearing you take the decision to dismiss an employee because he has committed an act of gross misconduct, use the **Dismissal without Notice Letter**.

PROCEDURES

You'll also find the Disciplinary and Grievance Procedures. These two procedures should play a pivotal role in how you deal with staff problems. If someone steps out of line, you both know what's expected by following the **Disciplinary Procedure**. But if you (allegedly) step out of line, the employee should invoke the **Employee Grievance Procedure**.

GRIEVANCES

Grievances are concerns, problems or complaints that employees raise with you. You should use a grievance procedure to deal with these complaints. Proper use of this procedure will enable you to deal with problems before they develop too far - often into constructive dismissal claims. Employees should aim to resolve most grievances informally with their line manager. If a grievance cannot be settled informally, the employee should raise it formally in accordance with your grievance procedure. There is now a statutory grievance procedure that employees must invoke if they subsequently wish to use the grievance as the basis of certain applications to an employment tribunal. Under the statutory procedure, employees must:

- inform you of their grievance in writing

- be invited by you to a meeting to discuss the grievance, where the statutory right to be accompanied applies, and be notified in writing of the decision. The employee must take all reasonable steps to attend this meeting
- be given the right of appeal by you and invited to attend an appeal meeting if the employee feels the grievance has not been satisfactorily resolved and be notified of the final decision.

On receiving a formal grievance, you should use the **Notification of Grievance Meeting** to set up a grievance meeting. Following the meeting, use the **Letter Notifying Outcome of Grievance Meeting** to let the employee know your response to his grievance. If the employee lodges an appeal, set up an appeal meeting using the **Notice of Grievance Appeal Meeting** and then confirm the outcome of the appeal using the **Letter Following Grievance Appeal Meeting**.

DISCIPLINARY PROCEDURE

Whilst the Company does not intend to impose unreasonable rules of conduct on its employees, certain standards of behaviour are necessary to maintain good employment relations and discipline in the interest of all employees. The Company prefers that discipline be voluntary and self-imposed and in the great majority of cases this is how it works. However, from time to time, it may be necessary for the Company to take action towards individuals whose level of behaviour or performance is unacceptable.

This disciplinary procedure is in two parts. Section A generally applies to those employees who have less than one year's continuous employment with the Company, although the Company reserves the right to apply Section B instead to any such employee. Section B applies to those employees who have one or more years' continuous employment with the Company.

This disciplinary procedure is **entirely non-contractual** and does not form part of an employee's contract of employment.

Section A

Before taking a decision to dismiss an employee on the grounds of misconduct or poor performance, the Company will, as a general rule and subject to any permitted statutory exceptions, comply with the following procedure:

Stage 1: Notification of allegations

The Company will notify the employee in writing of the allegations against him or her and will invite the employee to a disciplinary meeting to discuss the matter. The Company will also notify the employee of the basis for the complaint of alleged misconduct or poor performance.

Stage 2: Disciplinary meeting

Having given the employee a reasonable opportunity to consider his or her response to the allegations, a disciplinary meeting will then take place at which the employee will be given the chance to state his or her case. The employee may be accompanied, if requested, by a trade union official or a fellow employee of his or her choice. The employee must take all reasonable steps to attend that meeting. Following the meeting, the employee will be informed of the Company's decision in writing and notified of his or her right to appeal against it.

Stage 3: Appeals

If the employee wishes to appeal against the Company's decision, he or she can do so to a Director of the Company within five working days of the decision. Appeals should be made in writing and state the grounds for appeal. The employee will be invited to attend an appeal meeting chaired by a senior manager or a Director. At the appeal meeting, the employee will again be given the chance to state his or her case and will have the right to be accompanied by a trade union official or a fellow employee of his or her choice. Following the appeal meeting, the employee will be informed of the appeal decision in writing. The Company's decision on an appeal will be final.

The Company reserves the right not to follow this Section A procedure in relation to the imposition of a period of suspension with pay on, or the issuing of a disciplinary warning to, any employee who has less than one year's continuous employment with the Company.

Section B

Minor faults will be dealt with informally through counselling and training. However, in cases where informal discussion with the employee does not lead to an improvement in conduct or performance or where the matter is considered to be too serious to be classed as minor, for example, unauthorised absences, persistent poor timekeeping, sub-standard work performance, etc the following disciplinary procedure will be used. At all stages of the procedure, an investigation will be carried out.

The Company will notify the employee in writing of the allegations against him or her and will invite the employee to a disciplinary hearing to discuss the matter. The Company will also notify the employee of the basis for the complaint of alleged misconduct or poor performance. Having given the employee a reasonable opportunity to consider his or her response to the allegations, a formal disciplinary hearing will then take place, conducted by a manager, at which the employee will be given the chance to state his or her case, accompanied if requested by a trade union official or a fellow employee of his or her choice. The employee must take all reasonable steps to attend that meeting. Following the meeting, the employee will be informed in writing of the Company's decision in accordance with the stages set out below and notified of his or her right to appeal against that decision. It should be noted that an employee's behaviour is not looked at in isolation but each incident of misconduct is regarded cumulatively with any previous occurrences.

Stage 1: Written warning

The employee will be given a formal WRITTEN WARNING. He or she will be advised of the reason for the warning, how he or she needs to improves their conduct or performance, the timescale over which the improvement is to be achieved, that the warning is the first stage of the formal disciplinary procedure and the likely consequences if the terms of the warning are not complied with. The written warning will be recorded but nullified after six months, subject to satisfactory conduct and performance.

Stage 2: Final written warning

Failure to improve performance in response to the procedure so far, a repeat of misconduct for which a warning has previously been issued, or a first instance of serious misconduct or serious poor performance, will result in a FINAL WRITTEN WARNING being issued. This will give details of, and grounds for, the complaint, how he or she needs to improve their conduct or performance, the timescale over which the improvement is to be achieved and warn that dismissal will probably result if the terms of the warning are not complied with. This final written warning will be recorded but nullified after twelve months, subject to satisfactory conduct and performance.

Stage 3: Dismissal

Failure to meet the requirements set out in the final written warning will normally lead to DISMISSAL with appropriate notice. A decision of this kind will only be made after the fullest possible investigation. Dismissal can be authorised only by a senior manager or a Director. The employee will be informed of the reasons for dismissal, the appropriate period of notice, the date on which his or her employment will terminate and how the employee can appeal against the dismissal decision.

Gross misconduct

Offences under this heading are so serious that an employee who commits them will normally be summarily dismissed. In such cases, the Company reserves the right to dismiss without notice of termination or payment in lieu of notice. Examples of gross misconduct include:

- any breach of the criminal law, such as theft and unauthorised possession of Company property, fraud, deliberate falsification of records or any other form of dishonesty

- wilfully causing harm or injury to another employee, physical violence, bullying or grossly offensive behaviour

- deliberately causing damage to the Company's property

- causing loss, damage or injury through serious carelessness

- wilful refusal to obey a reasonable management instruction

- incapacity at work through an excess of alcohol or drugs

- a serious breach of health and safety rules

- harassing or victimising another employee on the grounds of race, colour, ethnic origin, nationality, national origin, religion or belief, sex, sexual orientation, marital status, age and/or disability.

The above is intended as a guide and is not an exhaustive list.

Suspension

In the event of serious or gross misconduct, an employee may be suspended on full basic pay while a full investigation is carried out. Such suspension does not imply guilt or blame and will be for as short a period as possible.

Appeals

An employee may appeal against any disciplinary decision, including dismissal, to a Director of the Company within five working days of the decision. Appeals should be made in writing and state the grounds for appeal. The employee will be invited to attend an appeal hearing chaired by a senior manager or a Director. At the appeal hearing, the employee will again be given the chance to state his or her case and will have the right to be accompanied by a trade union official or a fellow employee of his or her choice. Following the appeal hearing, the employee will be informed of the appeal decision, and the reasons for it, in writing. The Company's decision on an appeal will be final.

NOTIFICATION OF DISCIPLINARY HEARING

Date .... *(insert date)*

Dear .... *(insert name of employee)*

The Company is considering taking disciplinary action against you. You are therefore required to attend a disciplinary hearing on .... *(insert date - which should be at least three days after the date of the letter)*. This gives you a reasonable opportunity to consider your response to the Company's position.

A full investigation of the facts surrounding the complaint(s) against you was made by ... . *(insert name)*. Having now completed that investigation, the allegations against you are as follows:

- *(List each of the allegations in full detail.)*

(Where discipline is for potential gross misconduct: In the Company's view, these allegations constitute gross misconduct.*)*

For your information, copies of the following documents are enclosed:

- *(List copies of all witness statements (which should be signed and dated) and any other supporting documentary evidence that the employer intends to produce and rely on at the disciplinary hearing.)*

These documents form the basis for the Company's complaint(s) and the Company will therefore rely on these documents in support of the allegations made against you.

If you would like to submit a written statement for consideration in advance of the hearing, you may do so. This should be forwarded to .... *(insert name)*. At the hearing, you will of course be given the full opportunity to explain your case and answer the allegations. You may ask questions, dispute the evidence, provide your own evidence and otherwise argue your case. You may also put forward any mitigating factors that you consider relevant to your case. Due consideration will be given to any factors or explanations which you raise when considering what, if any, disciplinary sanctions are to be imposed.

The disciplinary hearing will be chaired by .... *(insert name)*, and .... *(insert name)* will also be present to take an attendance note of the hearing.

You have the statutory right to be accompanied at the disciplinary hearing. Your companion may be either a work colleague or a trade union official of your choice. Your companion will be permitted both to address the hearing (but not to answer questions on your behalf) and to confer with you during the hearing. You should inform the chair of the hearing in advance of the identity of your chosen companion.

(Where the employee already has an active final written warning on file: As you already have an active final written warning on your personnel file, I must inform you that the outcome of this disciplinary hearing could result in your dismissal.*)*

(Where discipline is for potential gross misconduct: Since the Company views the allegations against you as gross misconduct, I must inform you that the outcome of this disciplinary hearing could result in your summary dismissal.*)*

If you or your chosen companion is unable to attend this disciplinary hearing, you are asked to contact . . . . *(insert name of contact)* as a matter of urgency so that an alternative date and time can be scheduled. You are required to take all reasonable steps to attend the hearing. Failure to attend without good reason could result in the hearing being held, and a decision being taken, in your absence. However, if you fail to attend through circumstances completely outside your control and which are currently unforeseeable, the Company will arrange another hearing. Thereafter, if you fail to attend for a second time, the hearing will be held, and a decision will be taken, in your absence.

After the disciplinary hearing, you will be informed in writing of the Company's decision.

Yours sincerely,

. . . .

For and on behalf of the Company

Enc

WRITTEN WARNING

Date . . . . *(insert date)*

Dear . . . . *(insert name of employee)*

Further to your disciplinary hearing on . . . . *(insert date)* regarding . . . . *(insert details of incident)*, this letter constitutes a formal written warning. A copy of this letter will be placed on your personnel file.

At the hearing you were given the statutory right to be accompanied and you chose to (waive this right/have in attendance . . . . *(insert name of trade union official or work colleague)*).

A full investigation of the facts surrounding the complaint against you was made by . . . . *(insert name)*. Having put the specific facts to you for your comment at the disciplinary hearing, it was decided that your explanation/excuse was not acceptable. For this reason, it was deemed appropriate to formally warn you in writing about the following aspects of your conduct which are, in the Company's view, unacceptable:

* *(List each of the complaints giving rise to the warning.)*

You now need to improve your conduct in the following ways:

* *(List how the employee needs to improve his conduct in relation to each of the complaints.)*

This written warning forms part of the formal disciplinary process and will remain active for a period of . . . . *(insert figure)* months. If, within this period there is further cause for dissatisfaction in respect of similar misconduct to that described above, more serious disciplinary action may be taken against you. The consequences could be a final written warning and, ultimately, dismissal. It is hoped that this warning will lead to a sufficient immediate improvement in your conduct so that such action will not be necessary.

You have the right to appeal against the Company's decision if you are not satisfied with it. If you do wish to appeal, you must inform the Company in writing in accordance with the Company's disciplinary procedure, a copy of which is attached for your information. If you do appeal, the Company will then invite you to attend an appeal hearing which you must take all reasonable steps to attend.

Hearing conducted by: . . . .

Yours sincerely,

. . . .

For and on behalf of the Company

N.B. The warning should be signed by the person who conducted the disciplinary hearing whenever possible.

Please sign and return a copy of this letter to indicate that you have received it and understand its contents.

Signed: . . . . *(insert name of employee)*

Date: . . . . *(insert date)*

FINAL WRITTEN WARNING

Date . . . . *(insert date)*

Dear . . . . *(insert name of employee)*

Further to your disciplinary hearing on . . . . *(insert date)* regarding . . . . *(insert details of incident)*, this letter constitutes a final written warning. A copy of this letter will be placed on your personnel file.

At the hearing you were given the statutory right to be accompanied and you chose to (waive this right/ have in attendance . . . . *(insert name of trade union official or work colleague))*.

A full investigation of the facts surrounding the complaint against you was made by . . . . *(insert name)*. Having put the specific facts to you for your comment at the disciplinary hearing, it was decided that your explanation/excuse was not acceptable. For this reason, and in consideration of a previous active written warning you received for similar misconduct, it was deemed appropriate to formally warn you in writing about the following aspects of your conduct which are, in the Company's view, unacceptable:

- *(List each of the complaints giving rise to the warning.)*

You now need to improve your conduct in the following ways:

- *(List how the employee needs to improve his conduct in relation to each of the complaints.)*

This final written warning forms part of the formal disciplinary process and will remain active for a period of . . . . *(insert number)* months. If, within this period there is further cause for dissatisfaction in respect of similar misconduct to that described above, it may result in your dismissal from employment. It is hoped that this warning will lead to a sufficient immediate improvement in your conduct so that such action will not be necessary.

You have the right to appeal against the Company's decision if you are not satisfied with it. If you do wish to appeal, you must inform the Company in writing in accordance with the Company's disciplinary procedure, a copy of which is attached for your information. If you do appeal, the Company will then invite you to attend an appeal hearing which you must take all reasonable steps to attend.

Hearing conducted by: . . . .

Yours sincerely,

. . . .

For and on behalf of the Company

N.B. The warning should be signed by the person who conducted the disciplinary hearing whenever possible.

Please sign and return a copy of this letter to indicate that you have received it and understand its contents.

Signed: . . . . *(insert name of employee)*

Date: . . . . *(insert date)*

CONFIRMATION OF NO FURTHER DISCIPLINARY ACTION

Date . . . . *(insert date)*

Dear . . . . *(insert name of employee)*

Further to your disciplinary hearing held on . . . . *(insert date)*, the Company has decided that no formal disciplinary action will be taken against you on this occasion.

You have the right to appeal against the Company's decision if you are not satisfied with it. If you do wish to appeal, you must inform the Company in writing within five working days of receiving this decision. If you do appeal, the Company will then invite you to attend an appeal hearing which you must take all reasonable steps to attend.

Hearing conducted by, ... *(insert name)*

Yours sincerely,

. . . .

For and on behalf of the Company

DISMISSAL WITH NOTICE LETTER
(MISCONDUCT)

Date . . . . *(insert date)*

Dear . . . . *(insert name of employee)*

Further to your disciplinary hearing on . . . . *(insert date)* regarding . . . .
. . . . *(insert details of incident)* on . . . . *(insert date of incident)*, this letter confirms
the termination of your contract of employment. You are entitled to receive . . . . *(insert
number)* (weeks/months) notice. You (are/are not) required to work out this notice period.
We therefore confirm that the effective date of termination of your employment will be . . .
. . . . . . *(insert date)*.

At the hearing you were given the statutory right to be accompanied and you chose to
(waive this right/ have in attendance . . . . *(insert name of trade union
official or work colleague)*).

A full investigation of the facts surrounding the complaint against you was made by . . . . . .
. . . . *(insert name)*. Having put the specific facts to you for your comment at the
disciplinary hearing, it was decided that your explanation/excuses were not acceptable. For
this reason, and in consideration of a previous active final written warning you received for
similar misconduct, the Company believes it is left with no alternative but to dismiss you
with notice on the ground of misconduct. The Company would refer you to the following
aspects of your conduct which are, in the Company's view, unacceptable and which have led
to your dismissal:

* *(List each of the complaints which have resulted in the employee's dismissal.)*

You will receive your P45 in due course and you will be paid the following:

* your normal salary up to the date of the termination of your employment

* a payment in lieu of your notice period since we do not require you to work out this period*

* a sum in respect of accrued but untaken annual leave entitlement*.

*(*Delete as appropriate)*

Please note that in accordance with your contract of employment, the Company reserves
the right to deduct from your final termination payment a sum in respect of any annual
leave taken in excess of your accrued entitlement as at your termination date.

You have the right to appeal against the Company's decision if you are not satisfied with it. If you do wish to appeal, you must inform the Company in writing in accordance with the Company's disciplinary procedure, a copy of which is attached for your information. If you do appeal, the Company will then invite you to attend an appeal hearing which you must take all reasonable steps to attend.

Hearing conducted by: . . . . *(insert name)*

Yours sincerely,

. . . .

For and on behalf of the Company

N.B. The letter confirming termination should be signed by the person who conducted the disciplinary hearing whenever possible.

DISMISSAL WITHOUT NOTICE LETTER
(GROSS MISCONDUCT)

Date . . . . *(insert date)*

Dear . . . . *(insert name of employee)*

Further to your disciplinary hearing on . . . . *(insert date)* regarding . . . . *(insert details of incident)* on . . . . *(insert date of incident)*, this letter confirms the termination of your contract of employment without notice with effect from . . . . *(insert date)*.

At the hearing you were given the statutory right to be accompanied and you chose to (waive this right/have in attendance . . . . *(insert name of trade union official or work colleague))*.

A full investigation of the facts surrounding the complaint against you was made by . . . . *(insert name)*. Having put the specific facts to you for your comment at the disciplinary hearing, it was decided that your explanation/excuses were not acceptable. For this reason, the Company believes it is left with no alternative other than to summarily dismiss you on the ground of gross misconduct. The gravity of your misconduct is such that the Company believes the trust and confidence placed in you as its employee has been completely undermined. The Company would refer you to the following aspects of your conduct which are, in the Company's view, unacceptable and which have led to your summary dismissal:

- *(List each of the gross misconduct complaints which have resulted in the employee's summary dismissal.)*

You will receive your P45 in due course and you will be paid the following:

- your normal salary up to the date of the termination of your employment

- a sum in respect of accrued but untaken annual leave entitlement.*

(*Delete as appropriate)

Please note that in accordance with your contract of employment, the Company reserves the right to deduct from your final termination payment a sum in respect of any annual leave taken in excess of your accrued entitlement as at your termination date.

You have the right to appeal against the Company's decision if you are not satisfied with it. If you do wish to appeal, you must inform the Company in writing in accordance with the Company's disciplinary procedure, a copy of which is attached for your information. If you do appeal, the Company will then invite you to attend an appeal hearing which you must take all reasonable steps to attend.

Hearing conducted by: . . . . *(insert name)*

Yours sincerely,

. . . .

For and on behalf of the Company

N.B. The letter confirming termination should be signed by the person who conducted the disciplinary hearing whenever possible.

NOTICE OF DISCIPLINARY APPEAL HEARING

Date . . . . *(insert date)*

Dear . . . . *(insert name of employee)*

We refer to your letter dated . . . . *(insert date)* in which you lodged an appeal against the (written warning/final written warning/termination of your contract of employment) confirmed to you in our letter dated . . . . *(insert date)*.

Your appeal against our disciplinary decision will be heard at an appeal hearing to take place on . . . . *(insert date)* at . . . . *(insert time)* at . . . . *(insert location)*. The appeal hearing will be chaired by . . . . *(insert name - an appeal should be heard by a senior manager or director not previously involved in the procedure)*.

You have the statutory right to be accompanied at the appeal hearing. Your companion may be either a work colleague or a trade union official of your choice. Your companion will be permitted to address the hearing and to confer with you during the hearing but they will not be permitted to answer questions on your behalf. You should inform the chair of the appeal hearing in advance of the identity of your chosen companion.

If you would like to submit a written statement detailing your grounds for appeal for consideration in advance of the appeal hearing, you may do so. This should be forwarded to . . . . *(insert name)*. At the appeal hearing, you will of course be given an opportunity to set out the detailed grounds for your appeal, including providing any new evidence or new facts on which you may wish to rely.

If you or your chosen companion is unable to attend this appeal hearing, you are asked to contact . . . . *(insert name of contact)* as a matter of urgency so that an alternative date and time can be scheduled. You are required to take all reasonable steps to attend the appeal hearing. Failure to attend without good reason could result in the hearing being held, and a decision being taken, in your absence. However, if you fail to attend through circumstances completely outside your control and which are currently unforeseeable, the Company will arrange another appeal hearing. Thereafter, if you fail to attend for a second time, the hearing will be held, and a decision will be taken on your appeal, in your absence.

After the hearing, you will be informed in writing of the Company's decision. Please note that the decision made following this appeal hearing will be final and there will be no further right of appeal against it.

Yours sincerely,

. . . .

For and on behalf of the Company

LETTER FOLLOWING DISCIPLINARY APPEAL HEARING

Date . . . . *(insert date)*

Dear . . . . *(insert name of employee)*

Further to the appeal hearing held on . . . . *(insert date)* relating to the (written warning/ final written warning/termination of your contract of employment) confirmed to you in our letter dated . . . . *(insert date)*, the Company has now taken a decision on your appeal, namely that the original disciplinary decision (is hereby upheld/is hereby revoked).

(This means the written warning/final written warning/decision to terminate your contract of employment stands).

OR

(This means the (written warning/final written warning) will not stand and will be removed from your personnel file).

OR

(This means your employment with the Company is reinstated as if you had never been dismissed and you should therefore return to work on . . . . *(insert date)*).

The reasons for this decision are as follows:

* *(List reasons for decision to uphold or revoke the original disciplinary decision.)*

You have now exercised your right of appeal under the Company's disciplinary procedure and this decision is final. If, however, you wish to discuss any aspect of this decision in further detail, you are asked to contact . . . . *(insert name)*.

Appeal hearing conducted by: . . . . *(insert name)*

Yours sincerely,

. . . .

For and on behalf of the Company

SUSPENSION LETTER

Date .... *(insert date)*

Dear .... *(name of employee)*

A number of serious allegations have been brought to our attention regarding your conduct in the workplace. We are under a duty to fully and properly investigate these allegations.

We are therefore suspending you with full pay pending the results of this investigation.

Please note suspension is standard procedure in matters of this nature and does not indicate guilt in any way. Suspension does not constitute disciplinary action. Disciplinary action will not necessarily result.

Once our investigations are complete, we will contact you again to inform you of what action, if any, we will be taking. In the meantime, we must ask you to refrain from entering the Company's premises and from contacting any of your fellow employees. You are also required to return to .... *(insert name)* your *(office keys / swipe card / pass card, etc. and to provide details of your computer password)* for the period of your suspension from duty.

Yours sincerely,

....

For and on behalf of the Company

N.B. This specimen letter is for use in cases of potential gross misconduct only.

NOTICE OF PERFORMANCE REVIEW MEETING

Date . . . . *(insert date)*

Dear . . . . *(insert name of employee)*

We would like you to attend a performance review meeting on . . . . *(insert date - which should be at least three days after the date of the letter)* at . . . . *(insert time)* at . . . . *(insert location)*.

In the Company's opinion, you are currently failing to perform to the Company's required standards in the following respects:

- *(List each of the employee's failings in full detail and set these against the required standards of performance.)*

For your information, copies of the following documents, which support the Company's opinion, are enclosed:

- *(List copies of any supporting documentary evidence that you intend to produce and rely on at the meeting.)*

The purpose of the meeting is to establish why you are not performing properly and what assistance, if any, the Company can offer to improve your performance. The Company will therefore consider whether you are being trained and supervised properly, whether you have the proper equipment and facilities to enable you to work to your maximum potential and whether you are fully aware of what the Company requires of you.

At the meeting, you will be given an opportunity to explain your position and to put forward any mitigating factors that you consider relevant to your case.

The meeting will be chaired by . . . . *(insert name)*, and . . . . *(insert name)* will also be present to take an attendance note of the meeting.

You have the statutory right to be accompanied at the meeting. Your companion may be either a work colleague or a trade union official of your choice. Your companion will be permitted both to address the meeting (but not to answer questions on your behalf) and to confer with you during the meeting. You should inform the chair of the meeting in advance of the identity of your chosen companion.

If you or your chosen companion is unable to attend this meeting, you are asked to contact . . . . *(insert name)* as a matter of urgency so that an alternative date and time can be scheduled. You are required to take all reasonable steps to attend the meeting. Failure to attend without good reason could result in the meeting being held, and a decision being taken on your performance, in your absence. However, if you fail to attend through circumstances completely outside your control and which are currently unforeseeable, the Company will arrange another meeting. Thereafter, if you fail to attend for a second time, the meeting will be held, and a decision will be taken, in your absence.

After the meeting, you will be informed in writing of the Company's decision.

Yours sincerely,

. . . .

For and on behalf of the Company

Enc

WARNING OF POOR PERFORMANCE

Date .... *(insert date)*

Dear .... *(insert name of employee)*

Further to your performance review meeting on .... *(insert date)*, this letter confirms the points agreed at that meeting. A copy of this letter will be placed on your personnel file.

At the meeting you were given the statutory right to be accompanied and you chose to (waive this right/ have in attendance .... *(insert name of trade union official or work colleague))*.

We discussed the following areas of your current performance where the Company is of the opinion that you are failing to meet the required and notified standards:

- *(Summary of performance issues discussed)*

In explaining your downturn in performance, you raised the following points:

- *(Summary of points raised by employed)*

For your information, we enclose a detailed job description setting out the level of performance expected for each task you undertake as part of your duties. It also sets out where you are falling short of the expected level of performance.

The Company would also like to offer you the following (internal/external) training: (list training to be given). If you think there are additional ways in which we can help you to improve your performance, please speak to .... *(insert name)*.

The Company is prepared to allow you period to improve of (three/six) months commencing on .... *(insert date)*. During this period, we will formally meet with you on a (fortnightly/monthly) basis to review your performance and to discuss what, if any, progress or improvement you have made.

If you have failed to make sufficient progress, you will be formally warned of this fact and details will be provided to you. We must also warn you that failure to reach the required standards by the end of the (three/six) month period is likely to result in your dismissal on the ground of poor work performance.

Prior to any dismissal decision, the Company will of course give consideration to offering you any suitable alternative employment within your capabilities.

We hope that you will work with the Company to improve your performance so that further action will not be necessary.

You have the right to appeal against the Company's decision if you are not satisfied with it. If you do wish to appeal, you must inform the Company in writing in accordance with the Company's disciplinary procedure, a copy of which is attached for your information. If you do appeal, the Company will then invite you to attend an appeal meeting which you must take all reasonable steps to attend.

Meeting conducted by: . . . .

Yours sincerely,

. . . .

For and on behalf of the Company

N.B. The letter should be signed by the person who conducted the performance review meeting whenever possible.

Please sign and return a copy of this letter to indicate that you have received it and understand its contents.

Signed: . . . . *(insert name of employee)*

Date: . . . . *(insert date)*

EMPLOYEE GRIEVANCE PROCEDURE

Policy

The primary purpose of this grievance procedure is to enable staff to air any concerns that they may have about practices, policies or treatment from other individuals at work, and to produce a speedy resolution where genuine problems exist. It is designed to help all employees to take the appropriate action, when they are experiencing difficulties, in an atmosphere of trust and collaboration.

Although it may not be possible to solve all problems to everyone's complete satisfaction, this policy forms an undertaking by the Company that it will deal objectively and constructively with all employee grievances, and that anyone who decides to use the procedure may do so with the confidence that their problem will be dealt with fairly.

This grievance procedure is not a substitute for good day-to-day communication in the Company where we encourage employees to discuss and resolve daily working issues in a supportive atmosphere. Many problems can be solved on an informal footing very satisfactorily if all employees are prepared to keep the channels of communication between themselves open and working well. This procedure is designed to deal with those issues that need to be approached on a more formal basis so that every route to a satisfactory solution can be explored and so that any decisions reached are binding and long lasting.

Procedure

If you cannot settle your grievance informally, you should raise it formally. This procedure has been drawn up to establish the appropriate steps to be followed when pursuing and dealing with a formal grievance.

Stage 1

In the event of your having a formal grievance relating to your employment you should, in the first instance, put your complaint in writing and address it to your line manager. Where your grievance is against your line manager, your complaint should be addressed to an alternative manager or to the personnel department. A manager (who may not be the manager to whom your grievance was addressed) will then invite you to attend a grievance meeting to discuss your grievance and you have the right to be accompanied at this meeting by a trade union official or a fellow employee of your choice. Every effort will be made to convene the grievance meeting at a time which is convenient for you and your companion to attend. If this means that the meeting cannot be held within a reasonable period (usually within five working days of the original date set), we ask that you make arrangements with another companion who is available to attend. Any employee who is chosen to accompany another in a grievance hearing is entitled to take paid time off for this purpose.

You must take all reasonable steps to attend the grievance meeting.

Following the meeting, the Company will endeavour to respond to your grievance as soon as possible and, in any case, within five working days of the grievance meeting. If it is not possible to respond within this time period, you will be given an explanation for the delay and be told when a response can be expected. You will be informed in writing of the Company's decision on the grievance and notified of your right to appeal against that decision if you are not satisfied with it.

Stage 2

In the event that you feel your grievance has not been satisfactorily resolved, you may then appeal in writing to a Director of the Company within five working days of the grievance decision.

On receipt of your appeal letter, a more senior manager or a Director (who again may not be the person to whom your appeal was addressed) shall make arrangements to hear your grievance at an appeal meeting and at this meeting you may again, if you wish, be accompanied by a trade union official or a fellow employee of your choice.

You must take all reasonable steps to attend the grievance appeal meeting.

Following the meeting, the senior manager or Director will endeavour to respond to your grievance as soon as possible and, in any case, within five working days of the appeal hearing. If it is not possible to respond within this time period, you will be given an explanation for the delay and be told when a response can be expected. You will be informed in writing of the Company's decision on your grievance appeal.

This is the final stage of the grievance procedure and the Company's decision shall be final.

Former employees

Grievances may also be raised by ex-employees after their employment has ended. In this case, the grievance procedure set out above will continue to apply, unless both parties agree in writing that a modified form of grievance procedure will apply instead.

However, if your complaint relates to your dissatisfaction with a dismissal decision, you should not invoke the grievance procedure but should instead appeal against that decision in accordance with the appeal procedure with which you will have been provided.

NOTIFICATION OF GRIEVANCE MEETING

Date .... *(insert date of letter)*

Dear .... *(insert name of employee)*

We refer to your letter dated .... *(insert date)* in which you have lodged a formal grievance in accordance with the Company's grievance procedure.

You are now invited to attend a grievance meeting on .... *(insert date)* at ...... *(insert time)* at .... *(insert location)* at which your grievance will be discussed. At the grievance meeting, you will of course be given the full opportunity to explain your position. The grievance meeting will be chaired by .... *(insert name)*.

You have the statutory right to be accompanied at the grievance meeting. Your companion may be either a work colleague or a trade union official of your choice. Your companion will be permitted to address the meeting and to confer with you during the meeting but they will not be permitted to answer any questions on your behalf. You should inform the chair of the grievance meeting in advance of the identity of your chosen companion.

If you or your chosen companion is unable to attend this grievance meeting, you are asked to contact .... *(insert name)* as a matter of urgency so that an alternative date and time can be scheduled. You should take all reasonable steps to attend the grievance meeting. Failure to attend without good reason could result in the meeting being held, and a decision being taken, in your absence. However, if you fail to attend through circumstances completely outside your control and which are currently unforeseeable, the Company will then arrange another meeting. Thereafter, if you fail to attend for a second time, the meeting will be held, and a decision will be taken on your grievance, in your absence.

After the meeting, we will inform you in writing of the Company's decision on your grievance.

Yours sincerely,

....

For and on behalf of the Company

LETTER NOTIFYING OUTCOME OF GRIEVANCE MEETING

Date . . . . *(insert date of letter)*

Dear . . . . *(insert name of employee)*

Further to the grievance meeting held on . . . . *(insert date)*, the Company has now taken a decision on your grievance, namely that your grievance is (rejected/upheld/upheld in part).

(This means your grievance is not accepted as valid by the Company.)

OR

(This means your grievance is accepted as valid by the Company and therefore the Company will contact you shortly to let you know what steps it will be taking in response to this decision.)

OR

(This means only part of your grievance is accepted as valid by the Company, namely that part relating to . . . . *(insert details)*. Therefore, the Company will contact you shortly to let you know what steps it will be taking in response to this decision.)

The reasons for this decision are as follows:

- (List reasons for decision on the grievance.)

You have the right to appeal against the Company's decision if you are not satisfied with it. If you do wish to appeal, you must inform the Company in writing in accordance with the Company's grievance procedure, a copy of which is attached for your information. If you do appeal, the Company will then invite you to attend a grievance appeal meeting, which you must take all reasonable steps to attend.

Meeting conducted by: . . . . *(insert name)*

Yours sincerely,

. . . .

For and on behalf of the Company

NOTICE OF GRIEVANCE APPEAL MEETING

Date . . . . *(insert date of letter)*

Dear . . . . *(insert name of employee)*

We refer to your letter dated . . . . *(insert date)* in which you have lodged an appeal against the Company's decision on your grievance as confirmed to you in our letter dated . . . . *(insert date)*.

Your appeal against the Company's decision will be heard at an appeal meeting to take place on . . . . *(insert date)* at . . . . *(insert time)* at . . . . *(insert location)*. The appeal meeting will be chaired by . . . . *(insert name)*.

You have the statutory right to be accompanied at the grievance appeal meeting. Your companion may be either a work colleague or a trade union official of your choice. Your companion will be permitted to address the meeting and to confer with you during the meeting but they will not be permitted to answer any questions on your behalf. You should inform the chair of the appeal meeting in advance of the identity of your chosen companion.

If you or your chosen companion is unable to attend this appeal meeting, you are asked to contact . . . . *(insert name)* as a matter of urgency so that an alternative date and time can be scheduled. You should take all reasonable steps to attend the appeal meeting. Failure to attend without good reason could result in the meeting being held, and a decision being taken, in your absence. However, if you fail to attend through circumstances completely outside your control and which are currently unforeseeable, the Company will then arrange another meeting. Thereafter, if you fail to attend for a second time, the meeting will be held, and a decision will be taken on your grievance appeal, in your absence.

After the meeting, we will inform you in writing of the Company's decision. Please note that the decision made following this grievance appeal meeting will be final and there will be no further right of appeal against it.

Yours sincerely,

. . . .

For and on behalf of the Company

LETTER FOLLOWING GRIEVANCE APPEAL MEETING

Date . . . . *(insert date of letter)*

Dear . . . . *(insert name of employee)*

Further to the grievance appeal meeting held on . . . . *(insert date)*, the Company has now taken a decision on your grievance appeal, namely that the Company's original decision on your grievance (is hereby upheld/is hereby revoked).

(This means your grievance is still not accepted as valid by the Company.)

OR

(This means your grievance is now accepted as valid by the Company and therefore the Company will contact you shortly to let you know what steps it will be taking in response to this decision.)

The reasons for this decision are as follows:

* *(List reasons for decision to uphold or revoke the original decision on the grievance.)*

You have now exercised your right of appeal under the Company's grievance procedure and this decision is final.

Appeal meeting conducted by: . . . . *(insert name)*

Yours sincerely,

. . . .

For and on behalf of the Company

Section V

Sickness absence

Sickness absence

Employers must expect a certain amount of staff sickness absence. Most employees will require a few days off occasionally for illness. However, what should you do when faced with a persistent absenteeism problem or long-term incapacity?

PERSISTENT ABSENTEEISM.

If you have an employee who takes a lot of odd days off sick, it is important not to let the situation drift. When an employee's absence record reaches an unacceptable level, you should:

- review his attendance record. When employees are off work due to illness, always ensure he completes a ***Self-Certification of Sickness Absence Form*** on his first day back. This should include a section for the employee to record the reason for his absence

- investigate the reasons for each absence and request a further explanation from the employee

- where the employee produces no medical evidence to support his absence, ask him to consult his doctor to establish whether there is an underlying medical problem causing the level of absence. Obtain a medical report if necessary (see further below)

- if there is no underlying medical condition and the reasons for absence are unsatisfactory, then deal with the matter using your formal disciplinary procedure. As part of your procedure, give the employee the opportunity to make representations to explain his absences, tell the employee what level of improvement in attendance is required, the period within which that is to be achieved and what the consequences will be if there is insufficient improvement

- thereafter, monitor absence levels closely to see whether absence reduces to a reasonable level. If it does not, continue with your disciplinary procedure.

Although after a certain level of absence you can draw the line, there is no set number of days after which disciplinary action, and ultimately dismissal, becomes fair. You must take account of the individual circumstances of the case and operate absenteeism rules reasonably and fairly. A failure to do this may make any subsequent dismissal unfair.

LONG-TERM INCAPACITY.

It is possible for you to dismiss an employee on the grounds of lack of capability due to long-term ill-health. However, before doing so, you must take all reasonable steps to find out the current medical position. This will involve obtaining, with the employee's consent, a medical report from his GP or consultant, using the *Letter to Doctor Requesting Medical Report*. Before making an application to the employee's doctor for a medical report, you must first notify the employee and request his consent in writing to the medical report being obtained. In doing this, you will need to provide an explanation of his rights under the Access to Medical Reports Act 1988. This Act gives individuals the choice as to whether or not to consent to your seeking a medical report and it also gives them the right of access to any medical report prepared about them by their GP or consultant before it is supplied to you. Use the *Letter Requesting Consent to Obtain Medical Report* and the *Medical Report Consent Form*. Alternatively, a doctor you appoint may examine the employee, but only with his consent.

Once you have properly informed yourself of the employee's current state of health and the prognosis for his future health, you should consider the requirements of your business, the employee's length of service and past sickness record and whether he could be offered alternative work or other duties more suitable to his state of health. You must also consult meaningfully with the employee before taking any decision on whether or not to dismiss him. This will necessitate having at least two meetings with the employee following receipt of the medical report. Use the *Letter Requesting Employee's Attendance at a Meeting Following a Period of Long-Term Incapacity* to invite the employee to a first meeting to discuss the medical report and the reasonable adjustments that could be made to enable the employee to return to work, such as alternative employment. Use the *Notification of Long-Term Incapacity Meeting* once you reach the point where you are contemplating the dismissal of the employee. The purpose behind such consultation is to weigh up the situation, balancing your business need to get the work done against the employee's need for time off in order to improve his health. If you do take the decision to dismiss the employee, having considered the medical evidence and having properly

consulted with him, the *Letter of Dismissal on Long-Term Incapacity Grounds* will help you.

A dismissal on long-term incapacity grounds must accord with the statutory dismissal and disciplinary procedures. This means, amongst other matters, the employee must be given a right of appeal against the dismissal decision. If the employee exercises his right of appeal, use the *Notification of Long-Term Incapacity Dismissal Appeal Meeting* to set up the appeal meeting and then advise the employee of the outcome of his appeal using the *Confirmation of Outcome of Long-Term Incapacity Dismissal Appeal Meeting*.

DISABILITY DISCRIMINATION.

As well as the possibility of an employee making a claim for unfair dismissal if he has one or more year's continuous employment, there is the added risk of the employee bringing a claim of disability discrimination under the Disability Discrimination Act 1995. The Act applies irrespective of the length of employment and it now applies to all employers (the "small employer" exemption has been abolished). A medical report may be helpful in establishing whether or not an employee has a disability within the meaning of the Act.

Disability is defined under the Act as "a physical or mental impairment which has a substantial and long-term adverse effect on an employee's ability to carry out normal day-to-day activities". A mental impairment includes an impairment resulting from or consisting of a clinically well-recognised mental illness, for example mentioned in the World Health Organisation's International Classification of Diseases. The effect of an impairment is long-term if it has lasted at least twelve months, or if it is likely to last at least that long, or if it is likely to recur if in remission. The impairment must affect the ability of an employee to carry out normal day-to-day activities, which means it must affect one or more of the following:

- mobility
- manual dexterity
- physical co-ordination
- continence
- ability to lift, carry or otherwise move everyday objects
- speech, hearing or eyesight
- memory or ability to concentrate, learn or understand
- perception of the risk of physical danger.

In considering what is an adverse effect, the fact that an employee can, with great effort, carry out the activity does not mean that his ability to carry it out has not been impaired. In addition, where the employee is on medication or his impairment is being controlled by medical treatment or the use of an aid, you must consider how the activity would have been affected without the medication or control.

WHAT IS DISABILITY DISCRIMINATION?

There are now three ways in which you might unlawfully discriminate against a disabled employee. These are:

* by treating them less favourably (without justification) than you treat or would treat other employees and this is for a reason related to their disability
* by less favourable treatment on the ground of their disability
* by failing to make reasonable adjustments.

A dismissal on long-term incapacity grounds could therefore amount to disability discrimination. As mentioned above, discrimination also occurs if you fail to comply with your duty of "reasonable adjustment" in relation to the disabled person. The size and resources of your business are relevant in considering whether you have made reasonable adjustments. Reasonable adjustments may include:

* adjusting your work premises
* re-allocating job duties
* transferring the employee to fill an existing vacancy
* altering the employee's work or training hours
* assigning the employee to a different place of work or training
* allowing the employee to be absent for treatment and/or rehabilitation
* arranging training or mentoring
* acquiring or modifying equipment
* modifying instructions or manuals
* modifying procedures for testing or assessments
* providing supervision or other support.

Finally, note that there is no limit on the compensation that can be awarded by an employment tribunal in respect of disability discrimination and the award can also include a sum in respect of damages for injury to feelings.

SELF-CERTIFICATION OF SICKNESS ABSENCE FORM

This form is to record sickness absence information and is to be completed by you on the first day of return to work and countersigned by your line manager. It must be completed for all periods of sickness absence of half a day or more.

If you are absent due to illness for more than seven consecutive calendar days, he must also provide a doctor's certificate.

Once completed, this form will be placed on your personnel file and retained for a period of three years. A separate record will also be kept of your attendance record. The latter will simply record days of sickness absence but will not give the reasons for the absence.

Full name of employee:
_____

Date on which you first became
unfit for work:
_____

Date on which you returned to work:
_____

Total number of working days
(including half-days) absent due to illness:
_____

Please give precise details of the
nature of your illness or injury –
"sick", "ill" or "unwell" is insufficient:
_____

Did you visit your doctor or seek other
medical advice in relation to this period   YES/NO
of illness or injury?
_____

If you did not visit your doctor or seek
other medical advice, please give the reason
why not:
_____

I declare that the information I have given on this form is true and I confirm that I am now fit to resume work. I understand that it is a serious disciplinary offence to provide false information on this form.

Name: . . . .   Name: . . . .
(insert name of employee) . . . .   *(insert name of line manager)*

Signed: . . . .   Signed: . . . .

Date: . . . .   Date: . . . .

LETTER TO DOCTOR REQUESTING MEDICAL REPORT

Date . . . . *(insert date)*

Dear . . . . *(insert name of doctor or consultant)*

We employ . . . . *(insert name of employee)* who is a patient of yours. We would like you to prepare a medical report on (his/her) current state of health and on the prognosis for (his/her) future health. We attach a signed medical report consent form and we confirm that the employee's rights under the Access to Medical Reports Act 1988 have been explained in writing to (him/her). You will see that (he/she) has indicated that (he/she) (wishes /does not wish) to see the medical report before it is sent to the Company.

For your information, the employee's sickness absence record for the past twelve months is as follows: . . . . *(insert details)*.

We would be obliged if you could answer the following questions as part of your medical report.

1. What is the precise nature of the employee's current illness and what treatment or medication is the employee presently receiving?

2. When did the employee first receive a diagnosis in relation to the illness?

3. What effect does the employee's illness have on (his/her) ability to carry out normal day-to-day activities and is any effect substantial?

4. When, in your expert opinion, will the employee be fully fit to resume (his/her) normal job duties for the Company?

5. If, in your opinion, the employee will never be fully fit to resume (his/her) normal job duties, what level of capacity may reasonably be expected from the employee and within what period of time?

6. Given the nature of the illness and the normal job duties the employee is expected to perform (see the attached list), what is the likelihood of a recurrence or continuance of this illness in the future?

7. In your opinion, is the employee likely to render regular service for the Company in the future? If not, how much time off work do you predict the employee is likely to need in the twelve months period following (his/her) return to work?

8. In your opinion, is the employee a disabled person for the purposes of the Disability Discrimination Act 1995?

9. Are there any specific recommendations you would like to make in order to assist the employee in returning to work?

OR

1. Have you been able to find any serious underlying medical condition that explains the employee's recent pattern of sickness absence?

2. If so, please report on what this medical condition is, taking into account the normal job duties the employee is expected to perform (see the attached list).

List of main job duties

To assist you in preparing the medical report, we confirm that the employee is employed by the Company in the position of . . . . *(insert job title)* and this position has the following main job duties and responsibilities: . . . . *(insert list of main duties and responsibilities, particularly those including physical or mental exertion or stress relevant to the illness).*

We look forward to your early reply and enclose a stamped addressed envelope for your convenience. Please could you contact . . . . *(insert name of contact)* if the medical report will be delayed for any reason.

Please also attach your fee note for the preparation of the medical report and we will settle this according to the BMA's recommended scale of fees.

Yours sincerely,

. . . .
(Insert signature and name of author)

Encs.

LETTER REQUESTING CONSENT TO OBTAIN MEDICAL REPORT

Date . . . . *(insert date of letter)*

Dear . . . . *(insert name of employee)*

We refer to your current long-term absence from work due to illness. You have been absent since . . . . *(insert date)*.

OR

We refer to your recent intermittent sickness absence record. In recent months, you have been absent on the following occasions: . . . . *(insert details)*.

In order to address your absence record fairly and reasonably, we would now like to obtain a full medical report on your current state of health and the prognosis for your future health from your GP or consultant. Where necessary, this may also need to refer to your medical history if this is relevant. In the circumstances, we would therefore ask you to complete the attached medical report consent form and return it to . . . . *(insert name of contact)* by no later than . . . . *(insert date)*. If we do not hear from you by this date, we will conclude that you are refusing your permission to our obtaining a medical report.

Note that we are required by law to seek your consent before being able to request a medical report from your GP or consultant. You are, of course, free to refuse to give us permission to approach your GP or consultant for a report. However, we must warn you that, in such circumstances, we may then be forced to make a decision about your future health and employment without the benefit of an expert medical opinion. This would not be a particularly satisfactory situation.

If you have a consultant who has been providing you with clinical care on an ongoing basis, then it is obviously preferable for the medical report to come from that person. Otherwise, it should come from your GP.

In requesting a medical report from your GP or consultant, we must advise that you have rights under the Access to Medical Reports Act 1988. They are as follows:

1. You have the right to have access to any medical report about you which has been prepared by a medical practitioner who has responsibility for your clinical care, for example your GP or a consultant whom you have been seeing.

2. You have the right to inspect or be supplied with a copy of the medical report before it is sent to the Company if you have indicated this on the medical report consent form. You are also able to request a copy of the medical report from the Company once we have received it.

3. Should you wish to have access to the medical report before it is sent to the Company, you should contact your doctor to arrange this within 21 days of the Company applying for the report.

4. Having seen the medical report, you have the right to request in writing that your doctor amend any part of the report which you believe to be incorrect or misleading. Should the doctor not agree with your opinion and refuse to amend the report, you may require him or her to attach a statement of your views to the report.

5. If you have seen the medical report, it will not be forwarded to the Company unless you give the doctor your further consent.

6. You will not be entitled to see any part of the medical report if:

   (i) your doctor believes that disclosing it to you could seriously harm your physical or mental health or that of others;

   (ii) it indicates the doctor's intentions in respect of yourself; or

   (iii) it reveals information about the identity of a third person, unless that person has consented or they are a health professional.

   If you are refused access to any part of the medical report, the doctor will tell you which of the above reasons applies and you will be entitled to see the remainder of the report. Your right to request to amend the report applies only to the part of it which is disclosed to you.

We look forward to your early reply and enclose a stamped addressed envelope for your convenience.

Yours sincerely,

. . . .

(Insert signature and name of author)

MEDICAL REPORT CONSENT FORM

To: . . . . *(insert name of contact)*

of . . . . *(insert name of Company)*

From: . . . . *(insert name of employee)*

of . . . . *(insert address of employee)*

I have received and understood the content of your letter dated . . . . *(insert date)*, which includes an explanation of my rights under the Access to Medical Reports Act 1988.

I hereby consent to the Company requesting a medical report on my medical history and current state of health from my GP or consultant. I accordingly provide details of my GP or consultant as follows:

Name: . . . .

Practice address: . . . .

. . . .

Telephone number: . . . .

I [do/do not] wish to see the medical report prior to it being sent to the Company. If I do wish to see it, I understand that I should communicate with my doctor within 21 days of the Company applying for the medical report in order to make arrangements for access.

Name: . . . . *(insert name of employee)*

Signed: . . . .

Date: . . . .

LETTER REQUESTING EMPLOYEE'S ATTENDANCE AT A MEETING FOLLOWING A PERIOD OF LONG-TERM INCAPACITY

Date . . . . *(insert date of letter)*

Dear . . . . *(insert name of doctor or consultant)*

We refer to your current long-term absence from work due to illness. You have been absent since . . . . *(insert date)*.

We have now received a medical report on your current state of health and the prognosis for your future health from your GP/Consultant.

In order to address your absence record fairly and reasonably, we would now like to have a meeting with you to discuss the contents of the medical report. We have provisionally scheduled this meeting for . . . . . . *(insert date)* at . . . . . . *(insert time)* at . . . . *(insert location)* with . . . . *(insert name of contact)*. If you are unable to attend this appointment, please contact . . . . *(insert name of contact)* as a matter of urgency in order to schedule an alternative meeting time. If your health is such that you would prefer to bring a representative to accompany you at this meeting, please notify . . . . *(insert name of contact)* and this can be arranged.

In discussing the contents of the medical report with you, the purpose of the meeting is to explore if, and when, you will be in a position to return to your job with the Company. If this is unlikely to be in the near future, we will explore with you whether there is an alternative position that could be offered to you which is more suitable to your state of health. We will also discuss whether there are any adjustments we could reasonably make to your work arrangements, work provisions, criteria or practices or work environment which might enable you to return to work in some capacity.

We look forward to seeing you at the meeting.

Yours sincerely,

. . . .

(Insert signature and name of author)

NOTIFICATION OF LONG-TERM INCAPACITY MEETING

Date . . . . *(insert date)*

Dear . . . . *(insert name of employee)*

I am writing further to our recent meeting on . . . . *(insert date)* at which we discussed the contents of the medical report that we have obtained from your GP/Consultant. As you know, we also discussed the reasonable adjustments that could be made to your work environment or to work provisions, criteria or practices in order to accommodate you and to enable you to return to work in any capacity. I attach an attendance note of our meeting for your information.

Taking into account the contents of the medical report and our discussions at that meeting, one of a range of options that the Company is currently considering is the termination of your employment on the grounds of long-term incapacity for work. However, before any decision of this nature is taken by the Company, we would like to invite you to attend a further meeting on . . . . *(insert date)* at . . . . *(insert time)* at . . . . *(insert location)* where this proposal will be discussed further with you. This should give you a reasonable opportunity to consider your response to the Company's position.

The meeting will be conducted by . . . . *(insert name)*. You have the right to be accompanied at the meeting. Your companion may be either a work colleague or a trade union official of your choice. Your companion will be permitted to address the meeting and to confer with you during the meeting but they will not generally be permitted to answer any questions on your behalf. However, if your health is such that you would prefer your chosen companion to play a more active role, please let us know and we will endeavour to accommodate this. You should inform the chair of the meeting in advance of the identity of your chosen companion.

If you or your chosen companion is unable to attend this meeting, you are asked to contact . . . . *(insert name)* as a matter of urgency so that an alternative date and time can be scheduled. You should take all reasonable steps to attend the meeting. Failure to attend without good reason could result in the meeting being held, and a decision being taken on your long-term incapacity, in your absence. However, if you fail to attend through circumstances completely outside your control and which are currently unforeseeable, the Company will then arrange another meeting. Thereafter, if you fail to attend for a second time, the meeting will be held, and a decision on your future employment will be taken, in your absence.

After the meeting, we will inform you in writing of the Company's decision.

Yours sincerely,

. . . .

(Insert signature and name of author)

LETTER OF DISMISSAL ON LONG-TERM INCAPACITY GROUNDS

Date .... *(insert date)*

Dear .... *(insert name of employee)*

We refer to your current long-term absence from work due to illness and our recent meetings on .... *(insert date)* and .... *(insert date)* at which we discussed the contents of the medical report dated .... *(insert date)* that we obtained from your GP/Consultant and our proposal to terminate your employment on the grounds of long-term incapacity for work.

It is with regret that we must now inform you that the Company has decided to terminate your employment on the grounds of long-term incapacity for work. As you know, you were warned in advance of our second meeting, and at the meeting itself, that this was one option the Company might have to consider. In reaching this difficult decision, we have taken into account:

- the nature and current effects of your illness

- the prognosis for your future health

- the length of your employment

- the nature of your job

- your past sickness record

- the needs of the Company

- whether you could be offered an alternative position with the Company more suitable to your state of health

- whether there are any adjustments we could reasonably make to your work arrangements, work provisions, criteria or practices or work environment which might have enabled you to return to work in some capacity.

We have also taken into account the points you raised at our meetings, which can be summarised as follows: .... *(insert summary of employee's comments)*.

You are entitled to receive .... *(insert number)* (weeks/months) notice of the termination of your employment. You (are/are not) required to work out your notice period (although we accept that you will remain on sick leave for the duration of your notice period). We therefore confirm that your date of termination of employment will be .... *(insert date)*.

You will receive your P45 in due course and you will be paid the following:

- any pay owing up to the date of the termination of your employment

- a payment in lieu of your notice period since we do not require you to work out this period*

- a sum in respect of accrued but untaken annual leave entitlement*

- an ex gratia payment of £ . . . . *(insert amount).**

*(*Delete as appropriate)*

You have the right to appeal against the Company's decision to terminate your employment if you are not satisfied with it. If you do wish to appeal, you must inform . . . . *(insert name of contact)* in writing within five working days of receiving this decision. If you do appeal, you will then be invited to attend an appeal meeting which you must take all reasonable steps to attend.

If a prospective employer requires a reference from us, the person making the request should make it in writing to . . . . *(insert name of contact)*. We would like to extend to you our best wishes for the future.

Yours sincerely,

. . . .

(Insert signature and name of author)

NOTIFICATION OF LONG-TERM INCAPACITY DISMISSAL APPEAL MEETING

Date . . . . *(insert date)*

Dear . . . . *(insert name of employee)*

We refer to your letter dated . . . . *(insert date)* in which you lodged an appeal against the termination of your employment on the grounds of long-term incapacity for work as confirmed to you in our letter dated . . . . *(insert date)*.

Your appeal against the Company's decision will be heard at an appeal meeting to take place on . . . . *(insert date)* at . . . . *(insert time)* at . . . . *(insert location)*. The appeal meeting will be chaired by . . . . *(insert name)*.

You have the right to be accompanied at the appeal meeting. Your companion may be either a work colleague or a trade union official of your choice. Your companion will be permitted to address the meeting and to confer with you during the meeting but they will not generally be permitted to answer any questions on your behalf. However, if your health is such that you would prefer your chosen companion to play a more active role, please let us know and we will endeavour to accommodate this. You should inform the chair of the appeal meeting in advance of the identity of your chosen companion.

If you or your chosen companion is unable to attend this appeal meeting, you are asked to contact . . . . *(insert name)* as a matter of urgency so that an alternative date and time can be scheduled. You should take all reasonable steps to attend the appeal meeting. Failure to attend without good reason could result in the meeting being held, and a decision being taken, in your absence. However, if you fail to attend through circumstances completely outside your control and which are currently unforeseeable, the Company will then arrange another appeal meeting. Thereafter, if you fail to attend for a second time, the meeting will be held, and a decision will be taken on your appeal, in your absence.

After the meeting, we will inform you in writing of the Company's decision. Please note that the decision made following this appeal meeting will be final and there will be no further right of appeal against it.

Yours sincerely,

. . . .

(Insert signature and name of author)

CONFIRMATION OF OUTCOME OF LONG-TERM INCAPACITY DISMISSAL APPEAL MEETING

Date . . . . *(insert date)*

Dear . . . . *(insert name of employee)*

Further to the appeal meeting held on . . . . *(insert date)* relating to the termination of your employment on the grounds of long-term incapacity for work confirmed to you in our letter dated . . . . *(insert date)*, the Company has now taken a decision on your appeal, namely that the original dismissal decision (stands/is hereby revoked and your employment with the Company is therefore reinstated as if you had never been dismissed).

The reasons for this decision are as follows:

. . . .

. . . .

. . . .

(List reasons for decision to uphold or revoke the original dismissal decision.)

You have now exercised your right of appeal and this decision is final.

Appeal meeting conducted by: . . . . *(insert name)*

Yours sincerely,

. . . .

(Insert signature and name of author)

Section VI

Work and parents

Work and parents

Both male and female employees now benefit from a wide range of "family-friendly" rights and, as a result, it's easy to be confused about how the provisions operate. Our "work and parents" documents will ensure you know how to deal with requests for time off for a whole host of family reasons.

FAMILY-FRIENDLY RIGHTS

Employees may now benefit from the following statutory "family-friendly" rights:

- maternity leave - female employees only
- parental leave
- paternity leave
- adoption leave
- time off for dependants
- to request flexible working arrangements.

MATERNITY LEAVE

There are two categories of maternity leave: ordinary maternity leave and additional maternity leave. The amount of time allowed for maternity leave is linked to the employee's length of service. All pregnant employees are entitled to 26 weeks' ordinary maternity leave. Women who have completed 26 weeks' continuous service with you by the 15th week before their expected week of childbirth (EWC) are entitled to additional maternity leave as well. Additional maternity leave starts immediately after the end of ordinary maternity leave and continues for a further 26 weeks.

To take advantage of the right to maternity leave and statutory maternity pay (SMP) if eligible, a pregnant employee is required to notify you of her intention

to take maternity leave by the end of the 15th week before the EWC, unless this isn't reasonably practicable. However, she is able to change her mind about when she wants to start her maternity leave providing she informs you at least 28 days in advance. She is required to notify you that she is pregnant, when her EWC is and when she intends her maternity leave and SMP to start. The *Maternity Leave Plan* will ensure your employee complies with her notification requirements. There is also then a requirement on you to respond to your employee's notification of her leave plans within 28 days. You need to write to her, setting out the date on which you expect her to return to work if she takes her full entitlement to maternity leave. The *Acknowledgement of Notification of Maternity Leave Letter* provides a relevant precedent. It also covers the legal position regarding returning to work early i.e. before the end of the ordinary or additional maternity leave period. Note your employee does not have to give notice to you if she intends to return to work immediately after the end of her ordinary or additional maternity leave period. She can simply present herself for work on her due day of return.

PARENTAL LEAVE

Parental leave is a right for employees to take up to 13 weeks off work (18 weeks in the case of a disabled child) to look after a child or to make arrangements for the child's welfare. Both mothers and fathers, whether they are the natural or adoptive parents, qualify for parental leave, as long as either they are named on the child's birth certificate or they have parental responsibility for the child. Employees must have worked for you continuously for a year to qualify to take parental leave and it can be taken up until the child's fifth birthday or fifth anniversary of placement date for adoption (or 18th birthday if earlier). Parental leave is unpaid. Your employees can use the *Parental Leave Request Form* to make requests for parental leave.

There is a "fallback scheme" for parental leave which automatically applies in the absence of you having agreed your own scheme in a collective or workforce agreement and then having given that scheme legal force by writing it into your employees' contracts of employment. If no scheme has been agreed, the fallback scheme provides:

- leave must be taken in blocks of one week, up to a maximum of four weeks' leave in a year (for each child). If leave is to care for a disabled child, it may be taken a day at a time

- your employee must give 21 days' notice of parental leave (if leave is to be taken immediately after birth or adoption, 21 days' notice of the expected week of childbirth or the expected week of placement should be given)

- you can postpone parental leave for up to six months where the operation of your business would be unduly disrupted by the employee taking leave. You must confirm the postponement arrangements in writing no later than seven days after the employee's notice to take leave. The **Letter Postponing Parental Leave** will help you here. Note that leave cannot be postponed when an employee gives notice to take it immediately after the time the child is born or placed for adoption.

PATERNITY LEAVE

Eligible employees are able to take up to two weeks' paid paternity leave to care for their child or support the mother. To be eligible for paternity leave, an employee must have responsibility for the child's upbringing, be the biological father of the child or the mother's husband or partner and have worked continuously for you for 26 weeks as at the 15th week before the baby is due. Employees are entitled to take either one week or two consecutive weeks' paternity leave. It cannot be taken as odd days. Leave can start either from the date the child is born or from a chosen number of days or weeks after the date of childbirth. It must be completed either within 56 days of the date of childbirth or, if the child is born early, within the period from the date of childbirth up to 56 days after the expected date of childbirth. During paternity leave, most employees will be entitled to Statutory Paternity Pay (SPP).

Employees are required to inform you of their intention to take paternity leave by the 15th week before the expected week of childbirth, unless this isn't reasonably practicable. They need to tell you when the baby is due, whether they wish to take one or two weeks' leave and when they want their leave to start. Employees are able to change their mind about the date on which they want their leave to start providing that they tell you at least 28 days in advance. Employees have to give you a completed self-certificate as evidence of their entitlement to paternity leave and SPP. The **Paternity Leave Request Form** is the document for your employees to use to provide all the relevant information.

ADOPTION LEAVE

Adoption leave is available to individuals who adopt, or one partner of a couple where the couple adopt jointly. The couple may choose which partner takes adoption leave. The other half of the couple is entitled to take paternity leave. The right entitles eligible employees to take paid leave when a child is newly placed for adoption. To qualify for adoption leave, an employee must be newly matched with a child for adoption by an approved adoption agency and have worked continuously for you for 26 weeks as at the week in which they are notified of being matched with the child. Adopters are entitled to up to

26 weeks' ordinary adoption leave followed by up to 26 weeks' unpaid additional adoption leave. Most adopters will be entitled to Statutory Adoption Pay (SAP) during ordinary adoption leave.

Adopters can choose to start their leave from the date of the child's placement or from a fixed date which can be up to 14 days before the expected date of placement. Adopters are required to inform you of their intention to take adoption leave within seven days of being notified by their adoption agency that they have been matched with a child. They need to tell you when the child is expected to be placed with them and when they want their adoption leave to start. The **Adoption Leave Request Form** can be used to request the required information. Employees are able to change their mind about the date on which they want their leave to start providing that they tell their employer at least 28 days in advance. Employees have to give you a matching certificate from the adoption agency as evidence of their entitlement to adoption leave and SAP.

You have 28 days to respond to the employee's notification of their leave plans. You need to write to the employee, setting out the date on which you expect them to return to work if full entitlement to adoption leave is taken. Use the **Acknowledgement of Notification of Adoption Leave Letter** for this purpose. It also covers the legal position regarding returning to work early i.e. before the end of adoption leave. Your employee does not have to give notice to you if they intend to return to work immediately after the end of adoption leave. They can simply present themselves for work on their due day of return.

TIME OFF FOR DEPENDANTS

This is a right for all employees, regardless of length of service, to take a reasonable amount of time off work to deal with certain unexpected emergencies concerning a dependant and to make any necessary longer-term arrangements. Like parental leave, this is unpaid. The right covers the following:

- to provide assistance or make arrangements for the provision of longer-term care if a dependant falls ill, is injured or assaulted, or gives birth

- dealing with the consequences of the death of a dependant

- dealing with the consequences of a child being involved in an unexpected incident at school

- where childcare, or other dependant care arrangements, unexpectedly break down.

A "dependant" is a spouse, child, parent or a person living in the employee's household as part of their family but it doesn't include tenants or live-in employees. In cases of illness, injury or where care arrangements break down, a dependant may also be someone who reasonably relies on the employee for assistance. There is no set limit to the amount of time off which can be taken. In most cases, it will be one or two days at most, but this will depend on individual circumstances. Leave should be enough to help the employee cope with the crisis. The **Family Emergencies Absence Form** can be used to record absences falling under this statutory provision.

FLEXIBLE WORKING

Employees who are parents of young children have a right to request a change to their terms and conditions of employment to have flexible working arrangements to look after their children. This right to request flexible working can be exercised at any time up until shortly before the child's 6th birthday (or 18th birthday if the child is disabled). To be eligible to make a request, an employee must have worked for you for a continuous period of six months at the date the application is made. Employees can apply to vary the hours they work, the times they work or their place of work (between their home and your business). The provisions operate as follows:

- the employee makes a written request setting out the flexible working arrangement they seek: see the **Flexible Working Application Form**

- within 28 days of the application, you must set up a meeting with the employee to discuss it. The employee has a right to be accompanied at this meeting

- you must seriously consider the request and make a practical business assessment on whether flexible working can be arranged. You must then notify your decision to the employee within 14 days of the meeting

- if you accept the employee's request, you have to write to the employee, establishing a start date and providing a written note of the contract variation. The **Flexible Working Acceptance Letter** covers what you need to include

- if the application is refused, you must explain the grounds for refusal in writing and confirm the internal appeal procedure. Note you can only refuse an application on one of a number of specified grounds. These grounds are covered in the **Flexible Working Rejection Letter**

- the employee can appeal against a refusal within 14 days of the date of your rejection letter

- the employee cannot make a further application for twelve months.

ADOPTION LEAVE REQUEST FORM

You can use this form to request adoption leave under the right provided in law. Before completing this form, you should first check that you are eligible to make an adoption leave request. Further details on the adoption leave scheme, including eligibility requirements, can be found in the staff handbook under "adoption leave". For further information, you can also speak to . . . . *(insert name of contact)*.

It will help the Company to process your request if you provide as much information as you can about your request. It is important that you complete all the questions as otherwise your request may not be valid. Once you have completed the form, you should immediately forward it to . . . . *(insert name of contact)* and you should keep a copy for your own records.

Name of employee:

_____

Proposed date of commencement of adoption leave:

_____

Name and date of birth of the child:

_____

Date on which the child is expected to be placed for adoption (or, if the placement has already occurred, the date of placement):

_____

Date on which you were notified by the adoption agency of having been matched with the child:

_____

A copy of the matching certificate and adoption papers from the adoption agency should be attached in support of this request. If these documents are not yet available, they must be provided as soon as they are available.

Matching certificate and adoption papers attached?

YES/NO *(delete as appropriate)*

I declare that the information I have given on this form is true. I understand that it is a serious disciplinary offence to provide false information on this form.

Signed: . . . . *(insert name of employee)*

Date: . . . .

ACKNOWLEDGEMENT OF NOTIFICATION OF ADOPTION LEAVE LETTER

Date . . . . *(insert date)*

Dear . . . . *(insert name of employee)*

Thank you for letting us know that you will shortly be adopting a child and that you intend to take adoption leave commencing on . . . . *(insert date)*. I am now writing to tell you about your adoption leave and pay.

I confirm that, as we have discussed, you are eligible to take 52 weeks' adoption leave.

Given your chosen start date of . . . . *(insert date)*, your adoption leave will end on . . . . *(insert date)*.

If, at a later date, you wish to change the date your adoption leave starts you must notify . . . . *(insert name of contact)* by no later than 28 days before your proposed revised commencement date, or if that is not reasonably practicable, as soon as it is reasonably practicable for you to do so. Please contact . . . . *(insert name of contact)* if you wish to discuss this further.

As we also discussed, during your adoption leave, you are eligible to receive up to 26 weeks' Statutory Adoption Pay at the rate of £ . . . . *(insert amount)* per week.

OR

As we also discussed, you are not eligible to receive Statutory Adoption Pay during your adoption leave. The form SAP1 (enclosed) explains why you do not qualify for Statutory Adoption Pay. You should contact your adoption agency to find out if you can get any other financial help.

Given the dates of your adoption leave, you will be required to return to work on . . . . *(insert date which is day after adoption leave ends)*. If you wish to return to work before this date, you must give the Company at least 28 days' advance notice of the date on which you wish to return. If you fail to give sufficient notice, the Company will have the right to postpone your return date for a period equivalent to the unexpired portion of the 28 days' notice period, or until the end of your adoption leave period if that occurs earlier.

Finally, I would remind you that if you decide that you do not wish to return to work at the end of your adoption leave, you must still give us proper notice of termination of employment in accordance with your contract of employment. Your decision will not affect your entitlement to Statutory Adoption Pay.

If you have any questions about any aspect of your adoption entitlement, please do not hesitate to get in touch with . . . . *(insert name of contact)*. Congratulations and we wish you well.

Yours sincerely,

. . . .

(Insert signature and name of author)

FLEXIBLE WORKING APPLICATION FORM

You can use this form to make an application to the Company to work flexibly under the right provided in law to help eligible employees care for their children. Before completing this form, you should first check that you are eligible to make a request. For further information, please speak to .... *(insert name of contact)*.

You should note that under the right it may take up to 14 weeks to consider a request before it can be implemented and possibly longer where difficulties arise. You should therefore ensure that you submit your application to .... *(insert name of relevant person)* well in advance of the date you wish the request to take effect.

It will help the Company to consider your request if you provide as much information as you can about your desired working pattern. You can ask for changes to the number of hours you work, the times you work or the place you work. It is important that you complete all the questions as otherwise your application may not be valid. When completing the final two sections, you must think about what effect your change in working pattern will have both on the work that you do and on your work colleagues. Once you have completed the form, you should immediately forward it to .... *(insert name of relevant person)* and you should keep a copy for your own records. The Company then has 28 days after the day your application is received either to agree to your request or to arrange a meeting with you to discuss your request. If your request is granted, this will constitute a permanent change to your terms and conditions of employment unless otherwise agreed.

Name of employee:
_____

Department:
_____

Describe your current working pattern: (days/hours/time worked)

_____

Describe the working pattern you would like to work in the future:(days/hours/times worked).

_____

Date you would like the proposed new working pattern to start from:
_____

Impact of the new working pattern: (State how you think the proposed change in your working pattern will affect the Company and your work colleagues.)

_____

Accommodating the new working pattern: (State how you think the effect on the Company and your work colleagues can be dealt with.)

_____

I wish to apply to work a flexible working pattern that is different to my current working pattern under my right provided in law. I confirm that I meet each of the eligibility criteria as follows:

- I have responsibility for the upbringing of either a child under six or a disabled child under 18

- I am either the mother, father, adopter, guardian or foster parent of the child or I am married to or the partner of the child's mother, father, adopter, guardian or foster parent

- I am making this request to help me care for the child

- I am making this request no later than two weeks before the child's sixth birthday or 18th birthday where the child is disabled

- I have worked continuously as an employee of the Company for the last 26 weeks

- I have not made a request to work flexibly under this right during the past twelve months.

I declare that the information I have given on this form is true. I understand that it is a serious disciplinary offence to provide false information on this form.

Signed: . . . . *(insert name of employee)*

Date: . . . .

CONFIRMATION OF RECEIPT

To: . . . . *(insert name of employee)*

From:. . . . . *(insert name of contact at the company)*

I confirm that I received your request to change your work pattern on . . . . *(insert date)*. I shall be arranging a meeting to discuss your application within 28 days following this date. In the meantime, you might want to consider whether you would like a fellow work colleague to accompany you at the meeting.

Signed: . . . . *(insert name of contact)*

Date: . . . .

FLEXIBLE WORKING ACCEPTANCE LETTER

Date . . . . *(insert date)*

Dear . . . . *(insert name of employee)*

Following receipt of your flexible working application and our meeting on . . . . *(insert date)*, I have considered your request for a new flexible working pattern.

I am pleased to confirm that the Company is able to accommodate your application.

OR

Unfortunately, as explained to you at the meeting, the Company is unable to accommodate your original request. However, as we also discussed, I am able to offer you an alternative working pattern, which you agreed would be suitable to you.

Your new working pattern will be as follows: . . . . *(insert details of the new day / hours / times of work)*.

Your new working arrangements will begin from . . . . *(insert date)*.

Please note that the change in your working pattern represents a permanent change to your terms and conditions of employment and you have no right in law to revert back to your previous working pattern.

If you have any questions on the information provided in this letter, please contact . . . . *(insert name of contact)* to discuss them as soon as possible. Please sign the attached duplicate copy of this letter and return it to . . . . *(insert name of contact)* to signify your agreement to the changes set out above.

Yours sincerely,

. . . .
(Insert signature and name of author)

I accept the permanent change to my terms and conditions of employment set out in this flexible working acceptance letter dated . . . . *(insert date)*.

Signed: . . . .

Date: . . . .

FLEXIBLE WORKING REJECTION LETTER

Date .... *(insert date)*

Dear .... *(insert name of employee)*

Following receipt of your flexible working application and our meeting on ....*(insert date)*, I have considered your request for a new, flexible working pattern.

Unfortunately, having given full consideration to your application, I regret that the Company is unable to accommodate your request. The reasons for this are set out below.

You requested a reduction to your working hours/a change to the pattern of your working hours/a change to your place of work*. It is the Company's view that agreeing to these changes would:

- impose an unreasonable burden of additional costs on the Company*

- have a detrimental effect on the Company's ability to meet its customers' demands*

- have a detrimental impact on quality*

- have a detrimental impact on performance*

- create unacceptable difficulties for the Company as we have been unable to make arrangements to reorganise the work amongst the other staff*

- create unacceptable difficulties for the Company as we have been/would be unable to recruit additional staff*

- create unacceptable difficulties for the Company due to an insufficiency of work during the periods you proposed to work*

- be inappropriate due to structural changes the Company is planning.*

(*Delete as appropriate)

The business grounds listed above apply to your request for a new flexible working pattern because ....*(explain in more detail why the business grounds apply in the circumstances. An explanation of around two paragraphs will usually suffice).*

In addition, the other alternative work patterns we discussed at the meeting are inappropriate for the same reasons set out above.

If you are unhappy with the Company's decision to refuse your request for flexible working you have the right to appeal against it. If you wish to appeal, you must write to . . . . *(insert name of contact)*, setting out the grounds for your appeal, within 14 days of receipt of this letter. . . . . *(insert name of contact)* will then arrange a meeting with you to discuss your appeal within 14 days after receiving your appeal letter. After that meeting has been held, ... *(insert name of contact)* will then write to you within 14 days to notify you of the outcome of your appeal.

Yours sincerely,

. . . .

(Insert signature and name of author)

ACKNOWLEDGEMENT OF NOTIFICATION OF MATERNITY LEAVE LETTER

Date . . . . *(insert date)*

Dear . . . . *(insert name of employee)*

Thank you for letting us know about your pregnancy, the date your baby is due and that you intend to take maternity leave commencing on . . . . *(insert date)*. I am now writing to tell you about your maternity leave and pay.

I confirm that, as we have discussed, you are eligible to take 26 weeks' ordinary maternity leave.

OR

I confirm that, as we have discussed, you are eligible to take 26 weeks' ordinary maternity leave plus 26 weeks' unpaid additional maternity leave.

Given your chosen start date of . . . . *(insert date)*, your maternity leave will end on . . . . *(insert date)*.

If, at a later date, you wish to change the date your maternity leave starts you must notify . . . . *(insert name of contact)* by no later than 28 days before your proposed revised commencement date or 28 days before . . . . *(insert date leave starts)* (your original start date), whichever is sooner, or if that is not reasonably practicable, as soon as it is reasonably practicable for you to do so. Please contact . . . . *(insert name of contact)* if you wish to discuss this further.

As we also discussed, during your maternity leave, you are eligible to receive up to 26 weeks' Statutory Maternity Pay. Your maternity pay will be £ . . . . *(insert amount)* from . . . . *(insert date)* to . . . . *(insert date)* (which is 90% of your average weekly earnings) and then at the rate of £ . . . . *(insert amount)* per week from . . . . *(insert date)* to . . . . *(insert date)*.

OR

As we also discussed, you are not eligible to receive Statutory Maternity Pay during your maternity leave. The form SMP1 (enclosed) explains why you do not qualify for Statutory Maternity Pay. You may, however, be entitled to Maternity Allowance. If you take this form to your local Jobcentre Plus or Social Security Office, they will be able to tell you more.

Given the dates of your maternity leave, you will be required to return to work on . . . . *(insert date which is day after maternity leave ends)*. If you wish to return to work before this date, you must give the Company at least 28 days' advance notice of the date on which you wish to return. If you fail to give sufficient notice, the Company will have the right to postpone your return date for a period equivalent to the unexpired portion of the 28 days' notice period, or until the end of your maternity leave period if that occurs earlier.

As your employer, we want to make sure that your health and safety as a pregnant mother is protected while you are working and that you are not exposed to risk. We have already carried out a risk assessment to identify hazards in our workplace that could be a risk to any new, expectant, or breastfeeding mothers. Now you have told us you are pregnant, we will arrange for a specific risk assessment of your job and we will discuss what actions to take if any problems are identified. If you have any further concerns following this assessment and specifically in relation to your pregnancy, please let us know immediately.

Finally, I would remind you that if you decide that you do not wish to return to work at the end of your maternity leave, you must still give us proper notice of termination of employment in accordance with your contract of employment. Your decision will not affect your entitlement to Statutory Maternity Pay.

If you have any questions about any aspect of your maternity entitlement, please do not hesitate to get in touch with . . . . *(insert name of contact)*. Congratulations and we wish you well.

Yours sincerely,

. . . .
(Insert signature and name of author)

MATERNITY LEAVE PLAN

This plan covers your statutory rights to maternity leave and Statutory Maternity Pay (SMP). You do not have to fill in this plan to benefit from the right to maternity leave and SMP, but you do have to give the Company most of the information it contains. You may therefore wish to use this plan as a straightforward way of making sure you give the Company all the necessary information so that you can take maternity leave and receive SMP if you qualify for it. Once you have completed the plan, you should immediately forward it to . . . . *(insert name of contact)* and you should keep a copy for your own records.

Telling the Company that you are pregnant

You can tell us that you are pregnant as soon as you want to. This can be before you have decided when to take maternity leave. You will, of course, need to tell us if you want to take paid time off for antenatal appointments. The latest date you can inform us of your pregnancy is the 15th week before your expected week of childbirth (EWC).

Telling the Company when you want to take maternity leave

You must have told us by the 15th week before your EWC when you want to start your maternity leave and begin to receive SMP. This should be in writing. If you are using this plan for this purpose, you need to give it to us at the latest during the 15th week before your EWC. If you later wish to change the date on which you will start your maternity leave, you must give us at least 28 days' advance notice of your proposed revised start date.

Statutory Maternity Pay (SMP)

As well as qualifying for maternity leave, you may also qualify for SMP. If you do not qualify for SMP, you may be able to claim Maternity Allowance (MA) from the Benefits Agency.

How to use the plan

The plan is in four parts. Complete Part A first. This will help you decide how much maternity leave you can take and it will also tell you which parts of the rest of the plan you need to complete. Use Part D if you wish to return to work before you have taken your full maternity leave entitlement. Brief notes are given in the right hand column.

PART A - PLANNING MATERNITY LEAVE

To the Company

I am giving you this form to let you know that I am pregnant and to notify you of when I want to start my maternity leave and begin receiving SMP if I am eligible for it.

1. Your name: _____

2. The Company's name: _____

3. I am pregnant
YES/NO* *(*delete as appropriate)*

3. *See the notes above about telling the company that you are pregnant.*

4. My baby is due in the week beginning:
Sunday . . . . *(insert date of expected week of childbirth)*

4. *The expected week of childbirth is the week, beginning Sunday, in which it is expected you will have your baby.*

5. A certificate confirming this:
❏ Has been given to you already.
❏ Is enclosed with this form.
❏ Will be given to you shortly.

5. *If you qualify for SMP, you must give us a certificate giving the EWC at least 28 days before you wish to start your leave. The MATB1 form, which your doctor/midwife will give you, can be used.*

6. The 15th week before my expected week of childbirth is the week beginning:
Sunday . . . .

6. *Count back 15 weeks from the beginning of your EWC. This date is important for working out how much maternity leave you qualify for. All pregnant employees can take 26 weeks' ordinary maternity leave. If you have worked for the Company for at least 26 weeks on this date, you will also qualify for additional maternity leave.*

7. On this date I will have worked for the Company continuously for at least 26 weeks:
❏ Yes (go to Part C)
❏ No (go to Part B)

7. *Your length of employment usually runs from the first day you started work with the Company to the present day.*

PART B – ORDINARY MATERNITY LEAVE

Complete this section only if you answered NO to Question 7 in Part A. You only qualify for ordinary maternity leave. Ordinary maternity leave lasts for 26 weeks.

1. I intend to start my maternity leave on:
. . . . *(insert date)*

1. Start date: it is your decision when you start your maternity leave, but you cannot start it earlier than the 11th week before your EWC. You must notify us of your intended start date in the 15th week before the EWC.

2. If I am entitled to SMP, my Maternity Pay Period will start from:
Sunday . . . . *(insert date)*
(This is the date of the 1st Sunday after your answer in question 1)

2. Maternity Pay Period: the Maternity Pay Period is the 26 weeks period when you are entitled to receive SMP. It starts on the Sunday after you start your maternity leave. The latest it can start is the Sunday after the baby is due.

3. My ordinary maternity leave will finish on:
. . . . *(insert date)*

3. End of ordinary maternity leave: this is the end of the 26th week from when you start your maternity leave.

4. I am due back to work on:
. . . . *(insert date)*
I understand that if I want to return to work before this date, I must give you 28 days' advance notice of the date on which I want to return.

4. Date due back to work: if you qualify for ordinary maternity leave only, you are due back to work on the next working day after your ordinary maternity leave finishes.

You have now completed all the parts of the plan which apply to you. You should now sign the plan.

Signed: . . . . *(insert name of employee)*

Date: . . . .

PART C – ORDINARY AND ADDITIONAL MATERNITY LEAVE

Complete this section if you answered YES to Question 7 in Part A. You qualify for ordinary and additional maternity leave. Ordinary maternity leave lasts for 26 weeks. Additional maternity leave runs from the end of ordinary maternity leave for up to a further 26 weeks.

1. I intend to start my maternity leave on:
.... *(insert date)*

1. Start date: it is your decision when you start your maternity leave, but you cannot start it earlier than the 11th week before your EWC. You must notify us of your intended start date in the 15th week before the EWC.

2. If I an entitled to SMP, my Maternity Pay Period will start from:
Sunday .... *(insert date)*
(This is the date of the 1st Sunday after your answer in question 1)

2. Maternity Pay Period: the Maternity Pay Period is the 26 weeks period when you are entitled to receive SMP. It starts on the Sunday after you start your maternity leave. The latest it can start is the Sunday after the baby is due.

My additional maternity leave will run from the end of my ordinary maternity leave for up to 26 weeks.

Letting the company know when you are coming back to work: you do not have to tell us when you are due back to work. You are expected back at the end of your additional maternity leave.

3. My additional maternity leave will finish on:
.... *(insert date)*

3. End of additional maternity leave: this is the end of the 26th week from . when you start your additional maternity leave.

4. I am due back to work on:
.... *(insert date)*
I understand that if I want to return to work before this date, I must give you 28 days' advance notice of the date on which I want to return.

4. Date due back to work: you are expected back to work on the next working day after your additional maternity leave finishes.

You have now completed all the parts of the plan which apply to you. You should now sign the plan.

Signed: .... *(insert name of employee)*

Date: ....

PART D - RETURNING TO WORK EARLY

You will be expected back at the end of your full maternity leave entitlement. If you qualify for ordinary maternity leave only (so used Part B of the plan) you are due back on the date you put for question 4 of Part B. If you qualify for additional maternity leave (so used Part C of the plan) you are due back on the date you put for question 4 of Part C.

If you want to return earlier, you must give the Company at least 28 days' advance notice. This does not have to be in writing, but you may like to use this part of the plan to let us know.

I intend to return to work before the end of my maternity leave.
I intend to return to work on:................... *(insert date)*

You should now sign the plan and send Part D to the Company.

Signed: .... *(insert name of employee)*

Date: ....

FAMILY EMERGENCIES ABSENCE FORM

This form is to record information relating to time off taken to deal with family emergencies and is to be completed by you on your first day of return to work and countersigned by your line manager. Further details on the statutory right to time off for dependants can be found in the Staff Handbook.

Name of employee:
_____

Date on which you first took time off to deal with a family emergency: (If you had to leave the workplace early during the course of a working day, please state this and the time you left.)

_____

Date on which you resumed work:

_____

Total number of working days absent due to the family emergency:

_____

Please give precise details of the nature of the emergency:

_____

Please state the relationship of the dependant involved in the emergency to yourself:

_____

Please provide the reason for your absence i.e. why you in particular had to deal with the family emergency:

_____

Supporting documentary evidence of the   YES/NO
family emergency attached?
_____

I declare that the information I have given on this form is true. I understand that it is a serious disciplinary offence to provide false information on this form.

Signed: . . . .

(insert name of employee)

Signed: . . . .

(insert name of line manager)

Date: . . . .

Date: . . . .

PARENTAL LEAVE REQUEST FORM

You can use this form to request parental leave under the right provided in law to take time off work to help care for a child. Before completing this form, you should first check that you are eligible to make a parental leave request. Further details on the parental leave scheme, including eligibility requirements, can be found in the Staff Handbook under "parental leave". For further information, you can also speak to . . . . *(insert name of contact)*.

It will help the Company to process your request if you provide as much information as you can about your request. It is important that you complete all the questions as otherwise your request may not be valid. Once you have completed the form, you should immediately forward it to . . . . *(insert name of contact)* and you should keep a copy for your own records.

Name of employee:

_____

First date of proposed parental leave: (If leave is proposed to be taken immediately after birth or adoption, please provide the expected week of childbirth or the expected week of placement for adoption and state that this is the case.)

_____

Last date of proposed parental leave:

_____

Total number of working weeks of proposed parental leave:

_____

Name of the child and the child's date of birth or the date the child was first placed with you for adoption (if known at this stage):

_____

Is this child disabled (i.e. has disability living allowance been awarded)? If this child is disabled, please attach a copy of the letter awarding disability living allowance.	YES/NO/NOT YET KNOWN* *(*delete as appropriate)*

Please provide details of parental leave already taken in relation to this child (including relevant dates), whether in this employment or in the employment of a previous employer:

Please give any further information you would like your line manager to take into account in relation to this request:

_____

A copy of the child's birth certificate or adoption papers (as applicable) should be attached in support of this request. If these documents are not yet available, they must be provided as soon as they are available.

_____

Relevant supporting documents attached?   YES/NO*

                                                  (*delete as appropriate)

_____

I declare that the information I have given on this form is true. I understand that it is a serious disciplinary offence to provide false information on this form. I also accept that if I behave dishonestly in claiming an entitlement to parental leave, this will be viewed by the Company as a gross misconduct offence and could result in my summary dismissal. I recognise that the Company is entitled to make enquiries of any or all of my previous employers in relation to any previous periods of parental leave taken.

Signed: . . . . *(insert name of employee)*

Date: . . . .

APPROVAL OF PARENTAL LEAVE REQUEST

To: . . . . *(insert name of employee)*

From: . . . . *(insert name of contact at the Company)*

I confirm that I have received your request for parental leave. Your request for parental leave for . . . . *(insert number)* weeks from . . . . *(insert date)* to . . . . *(insert date)* is hereby approved.

Please note that parental leave is unpaid.

If you have any questions about any aspect of your parental leave entitlement, please do not hesitate to get in touch with . . . . *(insert name of contact)*.

Signed: . . . . *(insert name of employee)*

Date: . . . .

LETTER POSTPONING PARENTAL LEAVE

Date . . . . *(insert date of letter)*

Dear . . . . *(insert name of employee)*

Following receipt on . . . . *(insert date)* of your request to take parental leave from . . . . *(insert date)* to . . . . *(insert date)* and our meeting on . . . . *(insert date)*, I am writing to confirm that, as I informed you, unfortunately the Company is unable to accommodate your request for these dates because it considers that the operation of its business would be unduly disrupted if you were to take parental leave at the time you have requested. This is because:

- a significant proportion of the other employees in your department will already be on leave at this time*

- the period requested is during a time of peak demand at work*

- your role is such that your absence at this particular time would unduly harm the Company's business.*

(*Delete as appropriate)

The Company is able to postpone a period of parental leave but not for more than six months from the date on which you wanted it to start. In the circumstances, as we discussed, your postponed period of parental leave will be taken from . . . . *(insert date)* to . . . . *(insert date)* and your parental leave request form will be amended accordingly. The length of your postponed parental leave is equivalent to that in your original request.

If, as a result of this postponement, you now wish to withdraw your request for parental leave, you must contact . . . . *(insert name of contact)* as a matter of urgency.

For the avoidance of doubt, the Company is not able to postpone a period of parental leave which is to begin on the day on which your child is born or placed with you for adoption.

Yours sincerely,

. . . .

(Insert signature and name of author)

PATERNITY LEAVE REQUEST FORM

You can use this form to request paternity leave under the right provided in law to take time off work to help care for a child or support the child's mother or adopter. Before completing this form, you should first check that you are eligible to make a paternity leave request. For further information, please speak to . . . . *(insert name of contact)*.

It will help the Company to process your request if you provide as much information as you can about your request. It is important that you complete all the questions as otherwise your request may not be valid. Once you have completed the form, you should immediately forward it to . . . . *(insert name of contact)* and you should keep a copy for your own records.

Name of employee:

Date the baby is due to be born:

If the baby has already been born, please provide the actual date of birth:

In the case of an adopted child, the date on which the adoption agency told the adopter that they had been matched with the child:

In the case of an adopted child, the date on which the child is expected to be placed for adoption (or, if the child has already been placed, please provide the actual date of placement):

Date you would like your paternity leave (and statutory paternity pay if applicable) to start:

Do you wish to take one week's or two weeks' paternity leave:	One week/Two weeks* *(*delete as appropriate)*

Natural and non-adopted children

❏ Please tick here if you are completing this declaration.

I would like to take paternity leave and to receive statutory paternity pay if I qualify for it. I confirm that I meet each of the eligibility criteria as follows:

* I have, or will have, responsibility for the child's upbringing

* I am either the biological father of the child, or I am married to or living with the child's mother in an enduring family relationship, but I am not an immediate relative

* I am making this request for time off work to care for the child or support the child's mother

* I have worked continuously as an employee of the Company for 26 weeks by the week that falls 15 weeks before the week in which the child is/was expected to be born.

Adopted children

❏ Please tick here if you are completing this declaration.

I would like to take paternity leave and to receive statutory paternity pay if I qualify for it. I confirm that I meet each of the eligibility criteria as follows:

* I have, or will have, responsibility for the child's upbringing

* I am adopting the child jointly with my spouse/partner and I want to receive paternity leave and statutory paternity pay not adoption leave and statutory adoption pay, or I am married to the person adopting the child, or I am living with the person adopting the child in an enduring family relationship, but I am not an immediate relative

* I am making this request for time off work to care for the child or support the person adopting the child

* I have worked continuously as an employee of the company for 26 weeks up to and including the week I/the adopter was told by the adoption agency that I/they had been matched with the child.

I declare that the information I have given on this form is true. I understand that it is a serious disciplinary offence to provide false information on this form.

Signed: . . . . *(insert name of employee)*

Date: . . . .

APPROVAL OF PATERNITY LEAVE REQUEST

To: . . . .*(insert name of employee)*

From: . . . .*(insert name of contact at the Company)*

I confirm that I have received your request for paternity leave. Your request for paternity leave for [one week/two weeks] commencing on . . . . *(insert date)* is hereby approved. If, at a later date, you wish to change the date your paternity leave starts you must notify . . . . *(insert name of contact)* by no later than 28 days before your proposed revised commencement date, or if that is not reasonably practicable, as soon as it is reasonably practicable for you to do so.

[You are also entitled to receive Statutory Paternity Pay during your paternity leave. Statutory paternity pay is payable at the rate of £ . . . . *(insert amount)* per week or 90% of your average weekly earnings, whichever is less.]

If you have any questions about any aspect of your paternity leave entitlement, please do not hesitate to get in touch with . . . . *(insert name of contact)*.

Signed: . . . . *(insert name of contact)*

Date: . . . .

Section VII

Changing terms and conditions of employment

Changing Terms and Conditions of Employment

The best way to achieve a change to an employee's contract of employment, from both an employment law and a HR perspective, is by mutual agreement. But this may not always be possible. Therefore, in certain circumstances, you may have to consider other ways around the problem.

BINDING CONTRACT

The contract of employment is binding on both parties. This means that it's generally unlawful for you to change an employee's contract without the agreement of that employee. If you impose contractual changes on an employee without their express agreement, you will be acting in breach of contract.

EXPRESS AGREEMENT

If you wish to change an employee's contract of employment, you should first inform him both verbally and in writing that you are proposing (not making) a change. You should set out in detail the nature of the proposed change and why it's necessary for the needs of your business. The *Letter Seeking Agreement to Vary Terms of Contract of Employment* will help you here. The employee should be invited to consider the change and then revert to you with his views. If he's willing to accept the change, it can then be incorporated into his contract of employment and, for the avoidance of doubt, his consent should be obtained in writing. The best way to do this is to issue a new contract of employment for signature: use the *Letter Confirming Agreement to Vary Terms of Contract of Employment* for this purpose.

Note that if a variation of contract affects one of the terms and conditions required by law to be covered in the employee's written statement of employment particulars, then you must give the employee written notification of this as soon as possible, and, in any event, not later than one month after the change takes effect.

If an employee is not willing to accept a proposed change, you will have to engage in a period of negotiation to try and obtain his consent to the change. You could offer an incentive to help here. This could take the form of a pay increase, a one-off bonus or extra holiday entitlement. Alternatively, you might have to amend your proposal to one that is acceptable to the employee.

CONTRACTUAL POWER

If well-drafted, the contract of employment may include provisions allowing you to make certain changes to an employee's terms and conditions of employment without his consent, for example, requiring the employee to relocate to a different workplace. In the case of a change permitted by an express contractual provision, in most cases this will not constitute a variation of the terms of the contract and the change will therefore be lawful. This is subject to the proviso that you have proper business grounds for exercise of the express power. The *Variation of Terms of Contract of Employment Letter (In Exercise of a Contractual Power)* is the relevant precedent to use here. However, note that a provision which appears to permit you to change any provision of the contract in any manner that you like will be unenforceable as a matter of public policy. Employment tribunals will always look carefully at how widely the relevant clause has been drafted.

TERMINATION AND RE-EMPLOYMENT

If an employee refuses to agree to a change to his contract of employment, one option would be to terminate his current contract and then offer to re-engage him on the new terms and conditions. If there is a change that you must make to the contract for sound, good business reasons but the employee, having been consulted, will not agree to it under any circumstances, you may decide to give him notice that you are terminating the current contract. You would then offer immediate re-engagement on the new terms. The amount of notice must be the greater of the employee's contractual notice period and the statutory minimum notice period. Use the *Letter Terminating Employment and Offering Re-employment on New Terms* for this purpose.

This course of action is risky in the case of employees who have been employed by you for one year or more (although it is a safer option than imposing a unilateral variation to the terms of the contract - see further below). Even though you are terminating the current contract of employment with notice and therefore are not in breach of that contract, that termination still constitutes a dismissal and hence can still be an **unfair dismissal**. This is the case even if you have offered to re-engage the employee on new terms and he has indeed accepted that offer, albeit under protest. In defending this type

of claim, you will need to show a potentially fair reason for the dismissal, typically "some other substantial reason". The question will then be whether the dismissal was fairly conducted. In deciding whether a dismissal in these circumstances is fair or unfair, an employment tribunal will look at:

• your business reasons for wishing to vary the terms and conditions

• the consultation process you went through

• the efforts you made to reach a compromise

• the employee's reasons for objecting to the change.

The situation must be one where the only sensible alternative to an acceptance by the employee is to terminate the existing contract and offer a new one. There is no need for the alternative to be the survival of your business but you must have very good business reasons for the change and it must be a reasonable one to make in the circumstances. The tribunal will weigh the advantages to you of the change against the disadvantages to the employee. This is a balancing process. Where a change affects several staff, they will also look at whether a substantial proportion of the employee's colleagues agreed to the change.

Note that it is not necessary for you to go through the new statutory dismissal and disciplinary procedure where you are seeking to dismiss all the employees of a description or a category provided that you offer re-engagement before or on termination of the existing contracts of employment. However, where dismissal and re-engagement is only to affect one or a couple of employees, then unless they comprise all of the employees of a particular description or category, the statutory dismissal and disciplinary procedure will unfortunately still have to be followed. This requires the following three stages:

• you must set out in writing the circumstances which lead you to contemplate dismissing the employee. You must send this statement to the employee and invite him to attend a meeting, at which he has a right to be accompanied by either a trade union official or a work colleague, to discuss the matter

• the meeting must not take place until the employee has had a reasonable opportunity to consider his response to your letter. After the meeting, you must inform the employee of your decision and of his right to appeal against it

• if the employee wishes to appeal, he must inform you. You must then invite him to attend an appeal meeting. After the appeal meeting, you must inform him of your final decision.

Each step and action under this procedure must be taken without unreasonable delay. The timing and location of meetings must be reasonable and the employee must take all reasonable steps to attend the meetings. The meetings must be conducted in such a manner that enables both of you to explain your cases. Finally, in the case of appeal meetings, you should ensure you are represented by a more senior manager than attended the first meeting.

UNILATERAL VARIATION

Where an employee is not willing to accept a proposed change to his contract of employment, another option would be to impose it on him anyway. If he then continues to work under the new terms and conditions without making his objections known to you, after a period of time (usually months rather than weeks) he may be deemed to have accepted the change. The principle of deemed acceptance only applies to those provisions of the contract that are operative on a day-to-day basis where the variation has an obvious effect. Alternatively, the employee could work under the new terms and conditions under protest, in which case there is no acceptance by him, you are still in breach of contract and the employee can still issue a claim against you for this breach. Finally, you run the serious risk that, if your breach of contract is sufficiently fundamental, the employee will resign as a result of it and then claim constructive dismissal. Fundamental breaches include such matters as reductions in wages and working hours and probably changes to work location.

LETTER SEEKING AGREEMENT TO VARY TERMS OF CONTRACT OF EMPLOYMENT

Date . . . . *(insert date)*

Dear. . . . . *(insert name of employee)*

We refer to your contract of employment dated . . . . *(insert date)* and our meeting with you on . . . . *(insert date)* where we discussed a proposed change(s) to your contract of employment.

As we explained, the Company is proposing to make a change(s) to your contract of employment because *(set out the business reasons behind the proposed change(s)).*

As we also discussed, the details of the proposed change(s) are as follows:

* *(Set out in detail the nature of the proposed change(s), referring to the relevant provisions of the current contract of employment and the new provision of the proposed revised contract of employment.)*

For your consideration, we also enclose an amended draft contract of employment which incorporates the proposed change(s).

Please note that your continuity of employment with the Company will not be affected by any change to your contract of employment.

With your express consent, we would like the proposed change(s) to take effect on . . . . *(insert date).*

In the circumstances, we would ask you to fully consider the proposed change(s) and, with this in mind, we would like to have a further meeting with you to discuss any questions or concerns that you might have. Can we therefore ask you to meet *(insert name of contact)* on . . . . *(insert date)* at . . . . *(insert time)* at . . . . *(insert location).*

Alternatively, you might wish to simply accept the proposed change(s) without the need for a further meeting. If this is the case, could you please signify your acceptance to the change(s) detailed above by signing a copy of this letter and returning it to . . . . *(insert name of contact).*

Please be aware that the proposed change(s) will not be implemented without your express agreement. [In consideration for your agreement to the proposed change(s), the Company is willing to *(pay you a one-off lump sum payment of £x/increase your annual salary from £x to £x/increase your annual holiday entitlement from x days to x days, etc.).*]

Yours sincerely,

. . . .

(Insert signature and name of author)

Enc.

LETTER CONFIRMING AGREEMENT TO VARY TERMS OF CONTRACT OF EMPLOYMENT

Date . . . . *(insert date)*

Dear . . . . *(insert name of employee)*

We refer to your contract of employment dated . . . . *(insert date)*, our letter dated *(insert date)* and our meetings with you on . . . . *(insert date)* and . . . . *(insert date)*.

Following on from our meetings, we are writing to confirm your express agreement to the proposed change(s) to your contract of employment.

We therefore enclose two copies of your amended contract of employment. One copy is for you to keep. Could you please return the other copy, duly signed and dated, to . . . . *(insert name of contact)* by no later than . . . . *(insert date)* to formally confirm your acceptance of the change(s).

In the meantime, if you have any additional questions about your contract of employment or indeed on any other related matter, please do not hesitate to get in touch with . . . . *(insert name of contact)*.

Yours sincerely,

. . . .
(Insert signature and name of author)

Enc.

VARIATION OF TERMS OF CONTRACT
OF EMPLOYMENT LETTER
(IN EXERCISE OF A CONTRACTUAL POWER)

Date .... *(insert date)*

Dear .... *(insert name of employee)*

We refer to your contract of employment dated .... *(insert date)* and our meeting with you on .... *(insert date)* where we discussed a proposed change(s) to your contract of employment.

As we explained, the Company is proposing to make a change(s) to your contract of employment because *(set out the business reasons behind the proposed change(s)).*

As we also discussed, the details of the proposed change(s) are as follows:

- *(Set out in detail the nature of the proposed change(s), referring to the relevant provisions of the current contract of employment and the new provisions of the revised contract of employment.)*

We also enclose an amended draft contract of employment which incorporates the change(s). Please note that your continuity of employment with the Company will not be affected by any change to your contract of employment.

We would like the proposed change(s) to take effect on .... *(insert date).*

As you know, clause .... *(insert number)* of your contract of employment states that *(recite relevant clause which expressly permits the proposed change(s) to take place).*

This means that the proposed change(s) fall(s) directly within the ambit of the terms of your contract of employment. As such, the Company does not require your express consent to implement (it/them). That said, the Company does, of course, wish to take account of your views. In the circumstances, if there are any factors that you would like us to take into account which you think may influence our decision to implement the change(s), please contact .... *(insert name of contact)* by no later than .... *(insert date).* Unless we hear from you to the contrary, the proposed change(s) will take effect on .... *(insert date)* as detailed above and we will then issue you with an amended contract of employment.

If you have any additional questions about your contract of employment or indeed on any other related matter, please do not hesitate to get in touch with .... *(insert name of contact).*

Yours sincerely,

....

(Insert signature and name of author)

Enc.

LETTER TERMINATING EMPLOYMENT AND OFFERING RE-EMPLOYMENT ON NEW TERMS

Date . . . . *(insert date of letter)*

Dear . . . . *(insert name of employee)*

We refer to your contract of employment dated . . . . *(insert date)*, our general staff meeting on . . . . *(insert date)* and our individual meetings with you on . . . . *(insert date)* and . . . . *(insert date)* where we discussed a proposed change(s) to your contract of employment.

As we explained, the Company needs to make a change(s) to your contract of employment because *(set out the essential business / economic reasons behind the proposed change(s))*.

As we also discussed, the details of the change(s) proposed are as follows:

- *(Set out in detail the nature of the proposed change(s), referring to the relevant provisions of the current contract of employment and the new provisions of the revised contract of employment.)*

Throughout these meetings, the Company has fully explored with you whether a compromise agreement could be reached. You have consistently refused to accept the proposed changes or indeed to agree to any compromise that the Company has proposed. You stated that your reasons were *(insert summary of employee's reasons for refusing to accept the change(s) and answer any points made by the employee)*.

In the circumstances, and as we previously warned you in our last meeting, the Company has been left with no alternative but to terminate your contract of employment on the grounds of "some other substantial reason". In accordance with the terms of your contract of employment, you are entitled to receive . . . . . . *(insert figure)* (weeks/months) notice of the termination of your employment. You are required to work out your notice period. We therefore confirm that your date of termination will be . . . . *(insert date)*.

We also enclose an offer of employment on revised terms and conditions of employment to commence on . . . . . . *(insert date)*. That letter includes an amended contract of employment. If you wish to accept this offer, could you please complete the attached acceptance slip and sign and date the amended contract of employment and return the documentation to . . . . *(insert name of contact)* by no later than . . . . *(insert date)*. If we do not hear from you by this date, we will conclude that you are not willing to accept our new offer of employment and your employment will therefore end on . . . . *(insert date)* upon the expiry of your notice period. Please note that if you accept the offer of renewed employment, your continuity of service with the Company will be retained.

If you are at all unclear about the contents of this letter or you have any questions about the new offer of employment, please do not hesitate to get in touch with . . . . (insert name of contact).

[You have the right to appeal against the Company's decision to terminate your employment and offer you re-engagement if you are not satisfied with it. If you do wish to appeal, you must inform . . . . (insert name of contact) in writing within five working days of receiving this decision. If you do appeal, you will be invited to attend an appeal meeting which you must take all reasonable steps to attend.]

We look forward to hearing from you.

Yours sincerely,

. . . .

(Insert signature and name of author)

Enc

Section VIII

Redundancy

Redundancy

Redundancy law is much more complex than paying an employee off. There must be a genuine redundancy situation and you must treat the employee fairly in the procedure you use prior to the dismissal decision being taken. If you don't do things properly, you are at risk of an unfair dismissal claim. How can this be avoided?

DEFINITION

You cannot use redundancy as a tool to remove a poorly-performing or troublesome employee. According to the statutory definition of redundancy, there are four situations which could give rise to a redundancy:

- the closure of your business

- the closure of a place of work where the employee is employed

- a diminishing requirement for an employee to carry out work of a particular kind

- a diminishing requirement for an employee to carry out work of a particular kind at the place where an employee is employed.

If the reason for the redundancy fits into one of these categories, it will be a potentially fair reason to dismiss. However, it could be made unfair if you fail to follow a proper procedure. The principal procedural errors made by employers are firstly, lack of meaningful consultation, secondly, the unfair selection of an employee for redundancy and thirdly, failure to consider the employee for alternative employment that may be available. You must also ensure compliance with the statutory dismissal and disciplinary procedure if you are proposing to make less than 20 redundancies within a 90-day period. If you don't comply with the statutory procedure, the dismissal will be held to be automatically unfair if the employee has been employed for a year or more.

INDIVIDUAL CONSULTATION

You must carry out redundancy consultation with individual employees. This must take place irrespective of the number of proposed redundancies. A series of individual meetings with each of the affected employees should be held and this includes not only the ones who might be redundant, but those who are expected to stay. It is also best practice to hold a general staff meeting to discuss the reasons for the proposed redundancies. Consultation must be fair and should involve giving the employees a fair and proper opportunity to understand fully the matters about which they are being consulted and to express their views on those subjects.

Consultation should begin before you have reached a firm view as to whether redundancies should take place. You will no doubt have proposals as to which groups of employees are to be considered for redundancy, how employees are to be selected from within those groups and the number of employees who may need to be made redundant. These are typical matters that should be discussed as part of the consultation exercise. Volunteers for redundancy should be called for if possible. Use the *First Redundancy Consultation Letter* to ask for volunteers for redundancy, as well requesting the workforce to put forward their proposals to try and avoid the redundancy situation altogether.

One of the main purposes of consultation is to discuss the application of the redundancy selection criteria to the individual concerned. The employee should be given a fair opportunity to explain any factors which may influence your decision to select them for redundancy. Individual consultation also provides an opportunity to discuss with the employee the possibility of alternative employment within the business. Use the *Second Redundancy Consultation Letter* to outline the matters to be covered in consultation once provisional redundancy selections have been made and you are at the stage where dismissals are now being contemplated.

It is only when the consultation process has been completed that final decisions to dismiss can be made and confirmed in writing to employees: see the *Redundancy Termination Notice*. During the consultation process, any selection for redundancy should be clearly expressed to be provisional only.

The employee must be given a right of appeal against a redundancy dismissal decision. If the employee appeals, use the *Notification of Redundancy Appeal Meeting* to set up the appeal meeting and then use the *Confirmation of Outcome of Redundancy Appeal Meeting* to let the employee know the outcome of his appeal.

COLLECTIVE CONSULTATION

If you're proposing to make 20 or more redundancies within a 90-day period, you are under statutory obligations to consult with either recognised trade unions or, if there is no recognised trade union, with employee representatives and also to notify the Department of Trade and Industry. The provisions are too detailed to be discussed here but be aware of their existence and always seek specific legal advice where you're affected.

FAIR SELECTION

The selection criteria which you use to decide which employees are to be chosen for redundancy are of great importance. While you are given some latitude to tailor your staffing requirements to suit your business needs, you will fall foul of the law if these criteria are not objectively chosen and fairly applied. If you have agreed procedures providing criteria for redundancy selection, you should follow them. In determining the fairness of a redundancy dismissal, a tribunal will examine your pool for selection (the group of employees from whom those who were made redundant were drawn), the selection criteria which were applied to them and the manner in which you applied the criteria.

POOL FOR SELECTION

The pool for selection is likely to be those employees working in the area of your business where manning cuts are needed. You must not only consider the job descriptions of the employees but also what functions they perform in practice. You will probably be acting unreasonably if you exclude from the pool employees who are doing similar work to the group from which selections are made. The fact that one employee may be able to do another's job does not in itself mean that the employees hold similar positions, although if their jobs are interchangeable they should arguably be in the same pool (irrespective of job title or department). It may also be unreasonable if you treat employees working at two different sites or on two different shifts as separate groups for the purposes of redundancy selection.

SELECTION CRITERIA AND MANNER OF SELECTION

The selection criteria you choose must be both objective and necessary for the present and future needs of your business. Criteria should not be chosen with a view to ensuring certain unwanted members of staff are selected for redundancy! In selecting them, the starting point is to consider which factors are important and relevant to the future needs of your business. Once objective criteria have been decided upon, you must take care that any marks

the employee receives are verifiable by reference to evidence and data such as personnel files, attendance records, appraisal forms, disciplinary records, time sheets and skills audits. You must ensure that the relevant selection criteria are applied to the employees in a reasonable, fair and objective manner. The marks awarded in relation to each criterion cannot reflect your personal opinion. It is always prudent to have the marking system checked independently by at least two members of the management team to show that personal opinions aren't clouding judgement. Employees should be shown their individual marks as part of the consultation procedure so they can contest their selection at an early stage if they think it's unfair.

Examples of **objective selection criteria** include: length of service, attendance record, timekeeping record, disciplinary record, job performance, achievement of targets, relevant qualifications, relevant knowledge and skills, etc. Vague, subjective criteria such as inter-personal skills and attitude are generally, without the implementation of formal disciplinary measures, not acceptable. For a suitable precedent, use the **Selection Criteria**.

ALTERNATIVE WORK

During a redundancy programme, you may find that you're able to offer a redundant employee an alternative post within your business. In fact, in order to ensure a redundancy dismissal is fair, you should always explore whether there is any alternative work available. If the alternative post is "suitable" and the employee turns it down unreasonably, this can enable you to avoid liability to make a redundancy payment. In order to be suitable, the post must be on the same terms and conditions as the original post or suitable in relation to the particular employee. This is to be viewed objectively. On the other hand, the reasonableness of the employee's refusal depends on factors personal to him and is a subjective matter to be considered from his point of view. Always ask the employee to give detailed reasons for declining the post. This should enable you to assess whether a redundancy payment is due or not.

If the terms and conditions of the new post differ from those of the current post, the employee has a statutory trial period of four weeks in which to decide whether the alternative work is suitable for him. There are a number of statutory requirements to comply with here and the **Offer of Alternative Work** letter will ensure you follow the correct procedure.

REDUNDANCY PAYMENTS

If the employee that you're making redundant has been employed by you for two years or more, as a general rule he's entitled to a statutory redundancy payment. The exact amount of the redundancy payment is dependent on the employee's age, length of service (up to 20 years' service can count) and gross weekly wage. The latter is subject to a statutory cap on earnings, which is reviewed each year. Remember also that the employee will be entitled to the greater of their contractual notice or statutory minimum notice. See the redundancy payments *Ready Reckoner* to calculate how much is due.

FIRST REDUNDANCY CONSULTATION LETTER

Date . . . . *(insert date)*

Dear . . . . *(insert name of employee)*

We refer to the general staff meeting held on . . . . *(insert date)*. As we informed everyone at that meeting, the Company is in the regrettable position of having to consider implementing a redundancy programme as a result of (a downturn in work/a re-organisation of the Company's business and activities). At this early stage, we anticipate that it will be necessary to make . . . . *(insert number)* employees redundant (in the Company as a whole/in the department where you work).

As a first step, the Company wishes to invite employees to consider whether they would like to apply for voluntary redundancy. The terms available to those who apply and are accepted for voluntary redundancy can be obtained from . . . . *(insert name of contact)*. If you do wish to be considered for voluntary redundancy, please complete the attached application form and return it to . . . . *(insert name of contact)* by no later than . . . . *(insert date)*. If we do not hear from you by this date, we will conclude that you do not wish to volunteer for redundancy.

Please note that the Company reserves the right to decide whether or not to accept an employee's application for voluntary redundancy.

As part of the consultation procedure, we also wish to fully explore with employees whether there are options available other than redundancy in order to fulfil the Company's business needs. If you have any viable suggestions or proposals to put forward, please contact . . . . *(insert name of contact)* by no later than . . . . *(insert date)*.

If, after the applications for voluntary redundancy have been approved and other proposals put forward have been fully explored, there is still a need for the Company to make further redundancies, then the Company will have to consider implementing a compulsory redundancy programme.

Once this first stage of the consultation procedure has been completed, we will contact you again to discuss whether or not you may be affected by the redundancy programme.

Yours sincerely,

. . . .
(Insert signature and name of author)

SECOND REDUNDANCY CONSULTATION LETTER

Date .... *(insert date of letter)*

Dear .... *(insert name of employee)*

We refer to our general staff meeting on .... *(insert date)*, our first redundancy consultation letter dated .... *(insert date)* and our individual consultation meeting with you on .... *(insert date)*. We are now writing to summarise the current position in respect of the Company's redundancy programme.

As we have explained to you, the Company is in the regrettable position of having to implement a redundancy programme as a result of (a downturn in work in recent months/a re-organisation of the Company's business and activities). The Company has endeavoured to avoid the need for compulsory redundancies but this has not been successful. As you know, we asked for volunteers for redundancy and we have also fully investigated other measures as a means of avoiding redundancies, taking account of input received from employees. However, unfortunately, we are now in a position where we have to consider compulsory redundancies.

Taking account of any approved volunteers for redundancy, we now anticipate that it will be necessary to make ..... *(insert figure)* employees compulsorily redundant (in the Company as a whole/in the department where you work).

Having applied objective selection criteria, we must now advise you that you have been provisionally selected for redundancy. We would emphasise that this does not mean redundancy is a foregone conclusion. We want to explore with you whether there are any other alternative options available in order to avoid the redundancy situation, such as alternative employment within the Company.

[In this regard, we have currently identified the following options:

- *(Set out any options identified, for example, other vacancies within the Company, an agreed reduction in working hours, an agreed reduction in salary, etc.).*]

We would now like to have a further consultation meeting with you to discuss the Company's proposal and your provisional selection for redundancy before any final decisions are taken. This meeting has been scheduled for .... *(insert date)* at ...... *(insert time)* at .... *(insert location)* with .... *(insert name of contact)*.

In the meantime, we will continue to consider whether there are any further options that we can put forward for your consideration and we would ask you to do the same. It is important that you are fully involved in the consultation process. We are very keen to take account of your views and suggestions before reaching any final decisions on redundancy.

We would envisage at this stage that the consultation process will last at least one to two weeks (and will involve a couple of further meetings with you), although, depending on the course of events, it could last longer.

You have the right to be accompanied at the consultation meetings. Your companion may be either a work colleague or a trade union official of your choice. Your companion will be permitted to address the meeting and to confer with you during the meeting but they will not be permitted to answer questions on your behalf. You should inform the chair of the meeting in advance of the identity of your chosen companion.

For the avoidance of doubt, we confirm that we have used the following as our objective criteria for redundancy selection:

- *(List here the objective selection criteria.)*

We enclose the selection matrix as it relates to you. This sets out the marks you were awarded under each of the criterion. The matrix also includes a key explaining how the marking system works. Marking was carried out by . . . . *(insert name)* and . . . . *(insert name)*.

If you are of the opinion that the redundancy selection criteria may have been applied to you unfairly or that we have failed to take account of factors which you think may influence our decision to provisionally select you for redundancy, you should discuss this with . . . . *(insert name of contact)* as a matter of urgency.

If you or your chosen companion is unable to attend the scheduled consultation meeting, you are asked to contact . . . . *(insert name)* as a matter of urgency so that an alternative date and time can be scheduled. You are reminded that you are required to take all reasonable steps to attend the consultation meeting. Failure to attend without good reason could result in the meeting being held, and a decision being taken, in your absence. However, if you fail to attend through circumstances completely outside your control and which are currently unforeseeable, the Company will arrange another consultation meeting. Thereafter, if you fail to attend for a second time, the meeting will be held, and a decision on possible redundancy will be taken, in your absence.

Yours sincerely,

. . . .

(Insert signature and name of author)

Enc

REDUNDANCY TERMINATION NOTICE

Date . . . . *(insert date of letter)*

Dear . . . . *(insert name of employee)*

We refer to our general staff meeting on . . . . *(insert date)*, our redundancy consultation letters dated . . . . *(insert date)* and . . . . *(insert date)* and our individual consultation meetings with you on . . . . *(insert date)* and . . . . *(insert date)*.

It is with regret that we must now inform you that your present role with the Company is redundant. This decision is due to the Company (experiencing a downturn in work in recent months/having carried out a reorganisation of its business and activities for essential economic reasons).

As you know, we have fully considered with you whether other vacancies exist within the Company, but unfortunately we are not at present in a position to offer you any alternative post to your redundant position.

You are entitled to receive . . . . . *(insert figure)* (weeks/months) notice of the termination of your employment. You (are/are not) required to work out your notice period. We therefore confirm that your date of termination on the grounds of redundancy will be . . . . *(insert date)*.

You will receive your P45 in due course and you will be paid the following:

your normal salary up to the date of the termination of your employment.

- a statutory redundancy payment of £ . . . . . *(insert amount)* calculated as follows: . . . . *(insert calculation)**

- a contractual redundancy payment of £ . . . . *(insert amount)**

- a payment in lieu of your notice period since we do not require you to work out this period*

- a sum in respect of accrued but untaken annual leave entitlement*

- an ex gratia payment as compensation for loss of your employment of £ . . . . . . *(insert amount)**.

* *(Delete as appropriate)*

Please note that in accordance with your contract of employment, the Company reserves the right to deduct from your final termination payment a sum in respect of any annual leave taken in excess of your accrued entitlement as at your termination date.

[During your notice period, you are entitled to take a reasonable amount of paid time off work to look for alternative employment and attend job interviews. Before taking any such time off, you should obtain the prior agreement of your line manager, who may ask to see evidence of your appointments. Between now and your termination date, we will also continue to seek alternative employment for you within the Company.]

[On your last day of work, you will be required to return all Company property in your possession, including any keys, swipe cards, office equipment, company documents and correspondence.]

You have the right to appeal against the Company's decision to make you redundant if you are not satisfied with it. If you do wish to appeal, you must inform . . . . *(insert name of contact)* in writing within five working days of receiving this decision. If you do appeal, you will be invited to attend a redundancy appeal meeting which you must take all reasonable steps to attend.

If a prospective employer requires a reference from us, the person making the reference request should make that request in writing to . . . . *(insert name of contact)*.

We would like to extend to you our best wishes for your future. If you think we can be of any assistance to you in obtaining new employment, please do not hesitate to contact . . . . *(insert name of contact)*.

Yours sincerely,

. . . .
(Insert signature and name of author)

NOTIFICATION OF REDUNDANCY APPEAL MEETING

Date . . . . *(insert date)*

Dear . . . . *(insert name of employee)*

We refer to your letter dated . . . . *(insert date)* in which you lodged an appeal against the termination of your employment on the grounds of redundancy as confirmed to you in our letter dated . . . . *(insert date)*.

Your appeal against the Company's decision will be heard at an appeal meeting to take place on . . . . *(insert date)* at . . . . . . *(insert time)* at . . . . *(insert location)*. The appeal meeting will be chaired by . . . . *(insert name)*.

You have the right to be accompanied at the appeal meeting. Your companion may be either a work colleague or a trade union official of your choice. Your companion will be permitted to address the meeting and to confer with you during the meeting but they will not be permitted to answer any questions on your behalf. You should inform the chair of the appeal meeting in advance of the identity of your chosen companion.

If you or your chosen companion are unable to attend this appeal meeting, you are asked to contact . . . . *(insert name)* as a matter of urgency so that an alternative date and time can be scheduled. You should take all reasonable steps to attend the appeal meeting. Failure to attend without good reason could result in the meeting being held, and a decision being taken, in your absence. However, if you fail to attend through circumstances completely outside your control and which are currently unforeseeable, the Company will then arrange another meeting. Thereafter, if you fail to attend for a second time, the meeting will be held, and a decision will be taken on your appeal, in your absence.

After the meeting, we will inform you in writing of the Company's decision. Please note that the decision made following this appeal meeting will be final and there will be no further right of appeal against it.

Yours sincerely,

. . . .

(Insert signature and name of author)

CONFIRMATION OF OUTCOME OF REDUNDANCY APPEAL MEETING

Date .... *(insert date)*

Dear .... *(insert name of employee)*

Further to the appeal meeting held on .... *(insert date)* relating to the termination of your employment on the grounds of redundancy confirmed to you in our letter dated ... . *(insert date)*, the Company has now taken a decision on your appeal, namely that the original redundancy dismissal decision (stands/is hereby revoked and your employment with the Company is therefore reinstated as if you had never been dismissed).

The reasons for this decision are as follows:

* *(List reasons for decision to uphold or revoke the original redundancy dismissal decision.)*

You have now exercised your right of appeal and this decision is final.

Appeal meeting conducted by: .... *(insert name)*

Yours sincerely,

....

(Insert signature and name of author)

SELECTION CRITERIA

It is the Company's policy that if the need for compulsory redundancies arises, selection for redundancy will be made solely on the basis of objective criteria. Those criteria will then be fairly, reasonably and consistently applied to the affected employees. Marking will be conducted by at least two members of the Company's management team.

The first issue the Company will consider is the relevant pool for selection. In most cases, the pool will comprise those employees working in the area of the Company's business where manning cuts are deemed to be necessary. The Company will consider not only the job descriptions of the potentially affected employees but also what functions they perform in practice.

Once the relevant pool for selection has been ascertained, the Company will then apply one or more of the following as objective selection criteria:

* length of service with the Company*

* attendance record (excluding absences relating to maternity leave, pregnancy-related illnesses and disabilities)*

* timekeeping record*

* disciplinary record for misconduct/poor performance*

* job performance*

* achievement of targets*

* relevant qualifications*

* relevant knowledge and skills*

* the ability to take on additional or new job duties and responsibilities.*

(*Delete or add to as appropriate.)

The chosen selection criteria will be capable of objective substantiation and verification by reference to evidence and data, such as personnel files, appraisal forms, skills audits, attendance records, time sheets and disciplinary records. In deciding which criteria will apply for a particular redundancy programme, the overriding consideration will always be the future needs of the Company's business. This means that a particular criterion may carry more weight than another criterion, even though both criteria may be applied.

Where an employee in the pool for selection is disabled, the Company will ensure that they are not put at any disadvantage on account of the application of the selection criteria. The Company will accordingly make reasonable adjustments to the selection procedure to remove any disadvantage that the disabled employee may otherwise have.

REDUNDANCY PAYMENTS READY RECKONER

To calculate the number of weeks' pay due, read off the employee's age and number of complete years' service.

At the time of publication the statutory maximum weekly pay figure was £270. So, someone aged, say, 56 with twelve years' service is entitled to a redundancy payment of £4,860 (18 x £270). Note that service before the age of 18 does not count.

	COMPLETE YEARS' SERVICE																		
	2	3	4	5	6	7	8	9	10	11	12	13	14	15	16	17	18	19	20
20	1.0	1.0	1.0	1.0	-	0.0	0.0	0.0	0.0	0.0	0.0	0.0	0.0	0.0	0.0	0.0	0.0	0.0	0.0
21	1.0	1.5	1.5	1.5	1.5	-	0.0	0.0	0.0	0.0	0.0	0.0	0.0	0.0	0.0	0.0	0.0	0.0	0.0
22	1.0	1.5	2.0	2.0	2.0	2.0	-	0.0	0.0	0.0	0.0	0.0	0.0	0.0	0.0	0.0	0.0	0.0	0.0
23	1.5	2.0	2.5	3.0	3.0	3.0	3.0	-	0.0	0.0	0.0	0.0	0.0	0.0	0.0	0.0	0.0	0.0	0.0
24	2.0	2.5	3.0	3.5	4.0	4.0	4.0	4.0	-	0.0	0.0	0.0	0.0	0.0	0.0	0.0	0.0	0.0	0.0
25	2.0	3.0	3.5	4.0	4.5	5.0	5.0	5.0	5.0	-	0.0	0.0	0.0	0.0	0.0	0.0	0.0	0.0	0.0
26	2.0	3.0	4.0	4.5	5.0	5.5	6.0	6.0	6.0	6.0	-	0.0	0.0	0.0	0.0	0.0	0.0	0.0	0.0
27	2.0	3.0	4.0	5.0	5.5	6.0	6.5	7.0	7.0	7.0	7.0	-	0.0	0.0	0.0	0.0	0.0	0.0	0.0
28	2.0	3.0	4.0	5.0	6.0	6.5	7.0	7.5	8.0	8.0	8.0	8.0	-	0.0	0.0	0.0	0.0	0.0	0.0
29	2.0	3.0	4.0	5.0	6.0	7.0	7.5	8.0	8.5	9.0	9.0	9.0	9.0	-	0.0	0.0	0.0	0.0	0.0
30	2.0	3.0	4.0	5.0	6.0	7.0	8.0	8.5	9.0	9.5	10.0	10.0	10.0	10.0	-	0.0	0.0	0.0	0.0
31	2.0	3.0	4.0	5.0	6.0	7.0	8.0	9.0	9.5	10.0	10.5	11.0	11.0	11.0	11.0	-	0.0	0.0	0.0
32	2.0	3.0	4.0	5.0	6.0	7.0	8.0	9.0	10.0	10.5	11.0	11.5	12.0	12.0	12.0	12.0	-	0.0	0.0
33	2.0	3.0	4.0	5.0	6.0	7.0	8.0	9.0	10.0	11.0	11.5	12.0	12.5	13.0	13.0	13.0	13.0	-	0.0
34	2.0	3.0	4.0	5.0	6.0	7.0	8.0	9.0	10.0	11.0	12.0	12.5	13.0	13.5	14.0	14.0	14.0	14.0	-
35	2.0	3.0	4.0	5.0	6.0	7.0	8.0	9.0	10.0	11.0	12.0	13.0	13.5	14.0	14.5	15.0	15.0	15.0	15.0
36	2.0	3.0	4.0	5.0	6.0	7.0	8.0	9.0	10.0	11.0	12.0	13.0	14.0	14.5	15.0	15.5	16.0	16.0	16.0
37	2.0	3.0	4.0	5.0	6.0	7.0	8.0	9.0	10.0	11.0	12.0	13.0	14.0	15.0	15.5	16.0	16.5	17.0	17.0
38	2.0	3.0	4.0	5.0	6.0	7.0	8.0	9.0	10.0	11.0	12.0	13.0	14.0	15.0	16.0	16.5	17.0	17.5	18.0
39	2.0	3.0	4.0	5.0	6.0	7.0	8.0	9.0	10.0	11.0	12.0	13.0	14.0	15.0	16.0	17.0	17.5	18.0	18.5
40	2.0	3.0	4.0	5.0	6.0	7.0	8.0	9.0	10.0	11.0	12.0	13.0	14.0	15.0	16.0	17.0	18.0	18.5	19.0
41	2.0	3.0	4.0	5.0	6.0	7.0	8.0	9.0	10.0	11.0	12.0	13.0	14.0	15.0	16.0	17.0	18.0	19.0	19.5
42	2.5	3.5	4.5	5.5	6.5	7.5	8.5	9.5	10.5	11.5	12.5	13.5	14.5	15.5	16.5	17.5	18.5	19.5	20.5
43	3.0	4.0	5.0	6.0	7.0	8.0	9.0	10.0	11.0	12.0	13.0	14.0	15.0	16.0	17.0	18.0	19.0	20.0	21.0
44	3.0	4.5	5.5	6.5	7.5	8.5	9.5	10.5	11.5	12.5	13.5	14.5	15.5	16.5	17.5	18.5	19.5	20.5	21.5
45	3.0	4.5	6.0	7.0	8.0	9.0	10.0	11.0	12.0	13.0	14.0	15.0	16.0	17.0	18.0	19.0	20.0	21.0	22.0
46	3.0	4.5	6.0	7.5	8.5	9.5	10.5	11.5	12.5	13.5	14.5	15.5	16.5	17.5	18.5	19.5	20.5	21.5	22.5
47	3.0	4.5	6.0	7.5	9.0	10.0	11.0	12.0	13.0	14.0	15.0	16.0	17.0	18.0	19.0	20.0	21.0	22.0	23.0
48	3.0	4.5	6.0	7.5	9.0	10.5	11.5	12.5	13.5	14.5	15.5	16.5	17.5	18.5	19.5	20.5	21.5	22.5	23.5
49	3.0	4.5	6.0	7.5	9.0	10.5	12.0	13.0	14.0	15.0	16.0	17.0	18.0	19.0	20.0	21.0	22.0	23.0	24.0
50	3.0	4.5	6.0	7.5	9.0	10.5	12.0	13.5	14.5	15.5	16.5	17.5	18.5	19.5	20.5	21.5	22.5	23.5	24.5
51	3.0	4.5	6.0	7.5	9.0	10.5	12.0	13.5	15.0	16.0	17.0	18.0	19.0	20.0	21.0	22.0	23.0	24.0	25.0
52	3.0	4.5	6.0	7.5	9.0	10.5	12.0	13.5	15.0	16.5	17.5	18.5	19.5	20.5	21.5	22.5	23.5	24.5	25.5
53	3.0	4.5	6.0	7.5	9.0	10.5	12.0	13.5	15.0	16.5	18.0	19.0	20.0	21.0	22.0	23.0	24.0	25.0	26.0
54	3.0	4.5	6.0	7.5	9.0	10.5	12.0	13.5	15.0	16.5	18.0	19.5	20.5	21.5	22.5	23.5	24.5	25.5	26.5
55	3.0	4.5	6.0	7.5	9.0	10.5	12.0	13.5	15.0	16.5	18.0	19.5	21.0	22.0	23.0	24.0	25.0	26.0	27.0
56	3.0	4.5	6.0	7.5	9.0	10.5	12.0	13.5	15.0	16.5	18.0	19.5	21.0	22.5	23.5	24.5	25.5	26.5	27.5
57	3.0	4.5	6.0	7.5	9.0	10.5	12.0	13.5	15.0	16.5	18.0	19.5	21.0	22.5	24.0	25.0	26.0	27.0	28.0
58	3.0	4.5	6.0	7.5	9.0	10.5	12.0	13.5	15.0	16.5	18.0	19.5	21.0	22.5	24.0	25.5	26.5	27.5	28.5
59	3.0	4.5	6.0	7.5	9.0	10.5	12.0	13.5	15.0	16.5	18.0	19.5	21.0	22.5	24.0	25.5	27.0	28.0	29.0
60	3.0	4.5	6.0	7.5	9.0	10.5	12.0	13.5	15.0	16.5	18.0	19.5	21.0	22.5	24.0	25.5	27.0	28.5	29.5
61	3.0	4.5	6.0	7.5	9.0	10.5	12.0	13.5	15.0	16.5	18.0	19.5	21.0	22.5	24.0	25.5	27.0	28.5	30.0
62	3.0	4.5	6.0	7.5	9.0	10.5	12.0	13.5	15.0	16.5	18.0	19.5	21.0	22.5	24.0	25.5	27.0	28.5	30.0
63	3.0	4.5	6.0	7.5	9.0	10.5	12.0	13.5	15.0	16.5	18.0	19.5	21.0	22.5	24.0	25.5	27.0	28.5	30.0
64	3.0	4.5	6.0	7.5	9.0	10.5	12.0	13.5	15.0	16.5	18.0	19.5	21.0	22.5	24.0	25.5	27.0	28.5	30.0

Section IX

Termination of employment

Termination of Employment

The law on termination of employment can differ according to how long the employee has worked for you. For employees with less than a year's service, termination can be relatively straightforward. Longer-serving employees are not so easy to deal with because they have unfair dismissal rights. This section shows the safest ways to deal with both groups.

EMPLOYEES WITH LESS THAN ONE YEAR'S CONTINUOUS EMPLOYMENT

As a general rule, employees who have worked for you for less than a year do not have the right to claim unfair dismissal. There is an ever-growing list of exceptions to this rule (these exceptions are known as the automatically unfair dismissal reasons) and so it is always wise to take legal advice on any dismissal. In addition, employees can claim they have been unlawfully discriminated against on the grounds of their sex, marital status, race, disability, sexual orientation, religion or belief irrespective of their length of employment. That said, the general legal position is that if you wish to dismiss an employee due to their poor performance, misconduct or as a result of redundancy in their first year of employment, the dismissal can be reasonably easy. For these employees, their only legal entitlements are to the statutory dismissal and disciplinary procedure (see below), their contractual notice period (or to pay in lieu if you do not wish them to work out this period), to all outstanding wages and to pay in lieu of accrued but untaken annual leave entitlement.

The statutory dismissal and disciplinary procedure came into force on October 1, 2004. It now requires all employers to introduce and operate a dismissal and disciplinary procedure (DDP) from day one of employment. The DDP predominantly applies to dismissals, including dismissal on the grounds of capability, conduct, redundancy, expiry of a fixed-term contract and compulsory retirement. It also applies to "relevant disciplinary action" taken on conduct or capability grounds which falls short of dismissal, such as demotion,

transfer, an extension of the probationary period, etc., but it does not apply to the issuing of disciplinary warnings. The three steps of the DDP are:

- you must set out in writing the employee's alleged conduct or characteristics or other circumstances which lead you to contemplate dismissing or taking relevant disciplinary action against the employee. This must be sent to the employee and the employee be invited to attend a meeting to discuss the matter

- the meeting must take place before any action is taken but must not take place unless you have informed the employee what the basis was for including in the written statement the grounds given in it and the employee has had a reasonable opportunity to consider his response to that information. The employee must take all reasonable steps to attend the meeting. After the meeting, you must inform the employee of your decision and notify him of the right to appeal against it if he is not satisfied with it

- if the employee does wish to appeal, he must inform you. You must then invite him to attend an appeal meeting. The employee must take all reasonable steps to attend the meeting. After the appeal meeting, you must inform the employee of your final decision.

If an employee's performance or conduct has been unsatisfactory from the outset and you wish to dismiss him at the end of his probationary period, the **Unsatisfactory Probationary Period Letter** followed by the **Dismissal at End of Probationary Period Letter** can be used in order to ensure compliance with the statutory dismissal and disciplinary procedure. If the employee completes any probationary period but then becomes unsatisfactory within the first year of employment as a result of his poor performance or misconduct, the **Notification of Potential Dismissal Meeting** followed by the **Dismissal on Notice due to Unsatisfactory Performance/Conduct Letter** should be used. If during the first year of their employment there is a need to make an employee redundant as a result of an economic downturn or a business re-organisation, the **Notification of Potential Redundancy Meeting** followed by the **Dismissal on Notice due to Redundancy Letter** will help you here.

In all cases, if the employee appeals against a dismissal decision, use the **Notification of Appeal Meeting** and the **Confirmation of Outcome of Appeal Meeting**.

The position may become more complicated if the employee's contract of employment provides a contractual disciplinary procedure governing misconduct or poor performance. If the procedure is contractual, this means

231

you have agreed to follow it irrespective of the length of service of the employee. However, if the procedure is clearly expressed to be non-contractual, then there should be no problem. The same principle would apply to a contractual redundancy procedure.

EMPLOYEES WITH MORE THAN ONE YEAR'S CONTINUOUS EMPLOYMENT

Where an employee has been employed by you for a year or more, he has the right to claim unfair dismissal. In order to defend an unfair dismissal claim, you would need to show both a potentially fair reason for dismissal (there are five of these) and that you treated the employee fairly in the dismissal procedure you followed. The three main potentially fair reasons for dismissal are misconduct, lack of capability (encompassing both poor performance and long-term incapacity) and redundancy. Given the complexities of the law in these areas, the recommended letters and documents have been dealt with separately in this book: see *Disciplinary and Grievance Procedures, Sickness Absence and Redundancy*.

STATEMENT OF REASONS FOR DISMISSAL

An employee is generally only entitled to receive written reasons for his dismissal where he has at least a year's continuous service. You are obliged to provide the reason within 14 days of being asked. However, where the employee is dismissed while pregnant or while on a period of maternity or adoption leave, she is entitled to a written statement of the reason for her dismissal without having to request it and regardless of her length of employment. Use the *Statement of Reasons for Dismissal*, which can be adapted to cover either scenario. If you unreasonably refuse to provide a written statement or it is inadequate or untrue, the employee can present a complaint to an employment tribunal. Note also that because a written statement can be used as evidence in tribunal proceedings, you should take care to ensure that the reason you give is the real reason for the employee's dismissal.

RESIGNATIONS

Dismissal is only one side of the coin. Many employees resign from their jobs every year for a variety of reasons, the main one being because they have secured alternative employment, which they perceive to be more advantageous, either financially or for career progression. In these circumstances, there is usually no dispute between employer and employee and the employee leaves on reasonably good terms.

However, there is sometimes more to a resignation than meets the eye, even though the employee's resignation letter says very little. The employee may be resigning because there has been a fundamental breach of his terms and conditions of employment or because there has been a breakdown in mutual trust and confidence between you. Where the employee has been employed for a year or more, then you are in constructive dismissal territory in these circumstances. It is therefore best practice to request that all resigning employees complete an *Exit Questionnaire*. In addition, hold a meeting with the employee following his resignation to discuss the reasons for his decision. Adopting these practices enables problems to be brought to light and hopefully resolved before the situation becomes irretrievable. It also enables you to gather information about employees' reasons for leaving which can provide you with invaluable data about your employment practices, management style, etc.

If the employee has no outstanding grievance or issue, then a resignation can be simply accepted using the *Response to Resignation*, although, strictly speaking, a resignation by an employee is a unilateral act so there is no need for acceptance. However, an acceptance letter in these terms ensures the position on leaving dates and payment of outstanding wages is clear. Sometimes, an employee will resign and ask to leave early in order that he can start his new job as soon as possible. You do not have to accept this request. However, if you do accept it, it's important to record the fact that this agreement not to work out the contractual notice period was mutual. Otherwise, it could be later argued that you forced the employee to leave early in order to deprive him of his notice monies for the unexpired period of his notice. Not only that, it could potentially convert the resignation into a dismissal. Use the *Early Release from Notice Letter* for this purpose.

Sometimes an employee will resign "in the heat of the moment". This is common where there has been an argument at work and the employee's immediate response is to walk out. In addition, some resignation letters will be explicit and set out the employee's list of alleged grievances which has led to their resignation. It's common for this type of resignation letter to also state that the employee is leaving with immediate effect and will not be working out his notice period. In these circumstances, it's never safe to simply leave the position as it is because of the risk of a constructive dismissal claim. When either of these situations occur, the key is to make contact with the employee as a matter of urgency to try and resolve the issues which led to the resignation. This will necessarily involve meeting with the employee to discuss his problems or grievances. The *Response to "Heat of the Moment" Resignation* should be sent to the employee on the same day he either walked out or submitted his resignation.

Where the employee then raises a formal written grievance, you should follow a grievance procedure which complies with the new statutory grievance procedure. The relevant letters can be found elsewhere in this book: see *Disciplinary and Grievance Procedures*.

NEGOTIATED TERMINATIONS

Sometimes, it will become necessary to dismiss an employee in circumstances where you want to prevent him from issuing proceedings against you. This may happen in relation to senior employees when you do not propose to go through formal dismissal procedures because you want them out as soon as possible. In such circumstances, you should have a without prejudice meeting with the employee to discuss the termination package in return for his signing a *Compromise Agreement*. The without prejudice meeting should only take place with the employee's consent and he should be warned in advance that you wish to have a meeting of this nature. The employee is required by law to seek independent legal advice as to the terms and effects of a Compromise Agreement and, in particular, its effect on his ability to pursue his rights before an employment tribunal. You should ensure that all correspondence in connection with the negotiation of the agreement is marked "without prejudice" (see the *Letter to Accompany Compromise Agreement*) so as to avoid disclosure of it should negotiations for settlement break down prior to signature of the agreement. Marking correspondence this way will prevent the use of it in any subsequent legal proceedings. Bear in mind that if settlement negotiations do break down, you're likely to be left with a disgruntled employee!

UNSATISFACTORY PROBATIONARY PERIOD LETTER

Date . . . . *(insert date of letter)*

Dear . . . . *(insert name of employee)*

We refer to your offer of appointment letter dated . . . . *(insert date)* and your contract of employment dated . . . . *(insert date)*, both of which specified that your employment was on a (one/three/six) months probationary period.

We have carefully monitored your performance and conduct during your probationary period, which ended on . . . . *(insert date)*. As you are aware, it was necessary for . . . . *(insert name)* to speak to you on . . . . *(insert dates)* in connection with your (performance/conduct), which was viewed by the Company as unsatisfactory. You were given the opportunity to improve your (performance/conduct) during the remainder of your probationary period. However, the Company is of the view that you have still not attained the standards that it expects from you.

In the circumstances, now that your probationary period has come to an end, and having reviewed your performance and conduct, the Company is considering either dismissing you or extending your probationary period. The Company is contemplating this action having regard to the following aspects of your performance/conduct:

- *(List aspects of poor performance / conduct which have given rise to the proposal to dismiss the employee or to extend the probationary period.)*

However, before a decision is taken by the Company, you are invited to attend a meeting on . . . . . *(insert date)* at . . . . . . *(insert time)* at . . . . *(insert location)* where the proposal to dismiss you or to extend your probationary period will be discussed further. This gives you a reasonable opportunity to consider your response to the Company's position.

For your information, copies of the following documents are enclosed:

- *(List copies of all witness statements and any other supporting documentary evidence that the employer intends to produce and rely on at the meeting.)*

These documents form the basis for the Company's complaint(s) and the Company will therefore rely on these documents in support of the proposal to either dismiss you or to extend your probationary period.

If you would like to submit a written statement for consideration in advance of the meeting you may do so. This should be forwarded to . . . . *(insert contact name)*. At the meeting, you will be given the full opportunity to explain your case. You may also put forward any mitigating factors which you consider relevant to your case.

The meeting will be chaired by . . . . *(insert name)*.

You have the statutory right to be accompanied at the meeting. Your companion may be either a work colleague or a trade union official of your choice. Your companion will be permitted to address the meeting and to confer with you during the meeting but they will not be permitted to answer questions on your behalf. You should inform the chair of the meeting in advance of the identity of your chosen companion.

If you or your chosen companion is unable to attend this meeting, you are asked to contact . . . . *(insert contact name)* as a matter of urgency so that an alternative date and time can be scheduled. You are required to take all reasonable steps to attend the meeting. Failure to attend without good reason could result in the meeting being held, and a decision being taken, in your absence. However, if you fail to attend through circumstances completely outside your control and which are currently unforeseeable, the Company will arrange another meeting. Thereafter, if you fail to attend for a second time, the meeting will be held, and a decision will be taken, in your absence.

After the meeting, you will be informed in writing of the Company's decision.

Yours sincerely,

. . . .

(Insert signature and name of author)

Enc

DISMISSAL AT END OF PROBATIONARY PERIOD LETTER

Date . . . . *(insert date of letter)*

Dear . . . . *(insert name of employee)*

Further to the meeting held on . . . . . . *(insert date)* regarding the Company's proposal to either dismiss you or to extend your probationary period, having reviewed your performance and conduct and having discussed the issues with you at the meeting, unfortunately we must advise you that the Company has now decided to terminate your employment.

At the meeting you were given the statutory right to be accompanied and you chose to (waive this right/have in attendance . . . .) *(insert name of work colleague or trade union official).*

You are entitled to receive . . . . . . *(insert number)* (weeks/months) notice of termination of your employment. You (are/are not*) required to work out your notice period. We therefore confirm that your date of termination will be . . . . . . *(insert date).*

You will receive your P45 in due course and you will be paid the following:

- your normal salary up to the date of the termination of your employment
- a payment in lieu of your notice period since we do not require you to work out this period*
- a sum in respect of accrued but untaken annual leave entitlement*.

(*Delete as appropriate)

Please note that in accordance with your contract of employment, the Company reserves the right to deduct from your final termination payment a sum in respect of any annual leave taken in excess of your accrued entitlement as at your termination date.

You have the right to appeal against the Company's decision if you are not satisfied with it. If you do wish to appeal, you must inform . . . . *(insert name of contact)* in writing within five working days of receiving this decision. If you do appeal, you will then be invited to attend an appeal meeting which you must take all reasonable steps to attend.

Yours sincerely,

. . . .

(Insert signature and name of author)

NOTIFICATION OF POTENTIAL DISMISSAL MEETING

Date . . . . *(insert date of letter)*

Dear . . . . *(insert name of employee)*

I am writing to advise you that, unfortunately, the Company is considering dismissing you. The Company is contemplating this course of action having regard to the following aspects of your current (performance/conduct):

- *(List aspects of poor performance / conduct which have given rise to the proposal to dismiss the employee.)*

However, before a decision is taken by the Company, you are invited to attend a meeting on . . . . . *(insert date)* at . . . . . *(insert time)* at . . . . *(insert location)* where the proposal to dismiss you will be discussed further. This gives you a reasonable opportunity to consider your response to the Company's position.

For your information, copies of the following documents are enclosed:

- *(List copies of all witness statements and any other supporting documentary evidence that the employer intends to produce and rely on at the meeting.)*

These documents form the basis for the Company's complaint(s) and the Company will therefore rely on these documents in support of the proposal to dismiss you.

If you would like to submit a written statement for consideration in advance of the meeting you may do so. This should be forwarded to . . . . *(insert contact name)*. At the meeting, you will be given the full opportunity to explain your case. You may also put forward any mitigating factors which you consider relevant to your case.

The meeting will be chaired by . . . . *(insert name)*.

You have the statutory right to be accompanied at the meeting. Your companion may be either a work colleague or a trade union official of your choice. Your companion will be permitted to address the meeting and to confer with you during the meeting but they will not be permitted to answer questions on your behalf. You should inform the chair of the meeting in advance of the identity of your chosen companion.

If you or your chosen companion is unable to attend this meeting, you are asked to contact . . . . *(insert contact name)* as a matter of urgency so that an alternative date and time can be scheduled. You are required to take all reasonable steps to attend the meeting. Failure to attend without good reason could result in the meeting being held, and a decision being taken, in your absence. However, if you fail to attend through circumstances completely outside your control and which are currently unforeseeable, the Company will arrange another meeting. Thereafter, if you fail to attend for a second time, the meeting will be held, and a decision will be taken, in your absence.

After the meeting, you will be informed in writing of the Company's decision.

Yours sincerely,

. . . .
(Insert signature and name of author)

Enc.

DISMISSAL ON NOTICE DUE TO UNSATISFACTORY PERFORMANCE/CONDUCT LETTER

Date . . . . *(insert date of letter)*

Dear . . . . *(insert name of employee)*

Further to the meeting held on . . . . . . *(insert date)* regarding the Company's proposal to dismiss you, having reviewed your (performance/conduct) and having discussed the issues with you at the meeting, the Company is of the view that you have not attained the standards that it expects from employees at your level. We have decided that your explanation/excuses for your poor (performance/conduct) are not acceptable in the circumstances.

For this reason, we must advise you that the Company has now decided to terminate your employment.

At the meeting you were given the statutory right to be accompanied and you chose to (waive this right/have in attendance . . . .) *(insert name of work colleague or trade union official).*

You are entitled to receive . . . . . *(insert number)* (weeks/months) notice of termination of your employment. You (are/are not) required to work out your notice period. We therefore confirm that your date of termination will be . . . . . *(insert date).*

You will receive your P45 in due course and you will be paid the following:

* your normal salary up to the date of the termination of your employment
* a payment in lieu of your notice period since we do not require you to work out this period*
* a sum in respect of accrued but untaken annual leave entitlement.*

(*Delete as appropriate.)

Please note that in accordance with your contract of employment, the Company reserves the right to deduct from your final termination payment a sum in respect of any annual leave taken in excess of your accrued entitlement as at your termination date.

You have the right to appeal against the Company's decision if you are not satisfied with it. If you do wish to appeal, you must inform . . . . *(insert name of contact)* in writing within five working days of receiving this decision. If you do appeal, you will then be invited to attend an appeal meeting which you must take all reasonable steps to attend.

Yours sincerely,

. . . .

(Insert signature and name of author)

NOTIFICATION OF POTENTIAL REDUNDANCY MEETING

Date . . . . *(insert date of letter)*

Dear . . . . *(insert name of employee)*

I am writing to advise you that, unfortunately, the Company is considering making you redundant. The Company is contemplating this course of action having regard to the following business circumstances:

* (Provide details of economic downturn or business restructuring which has given rise to the proposal to make the employee redundant.)

However, before a decision is taken by the Company, you are invited to attend a meeting with . . . . *(insert name)* on . . . . . . *(insert date)* at . . . . *(insert time)* at . . . . *(insert location)* where the proposal to make you redundant will be discussed further. This gives you a reasonable opportunity to consider your response to the Company's position.

You have the right to be accompanied at the meeting. Your companion may be either a work colleague or a trade union official of your choice. Your companion will be permitted to address the meeting and to confer with you during the meeting but they will not be permitted to answer questions on your behalf. You should inform the chair of the meeting in advance of the identity of your chosen companion.

If you or your chosen companion is unable to attend this meeting, you are asked to contact . . . . *(insert contact name)* as a matter of urgency so that an alternative date and time can be scheduled. You are required to take all reasonable steps to attend the meeting. Failure to attend without good reason could result in the meeting being held, and a decision being taken, in your absence. However, if you fail to attend through circumstances completely outside your control and which are currently unforeseeable, the Company will arrange another meeting. Thereafter, if you fail to attend for a second time, the meeting will be held, and a decision will be taken, in your absence.

After the meeting, you will be informed in writing of the Company's decision.

Yours sincerely,

. . . .

(Insert signature and name of author)

DISMISSAL ON NOTICE DUE TO REDUNDANCY LETTER

Date . . . . *(insert date of letter)*

Dear . . . . *(insert name of employee)*

We refer to our meeting on . . . . . *(insert date)* when we discussed the Company's proposal to dismiss you on the grounds of redundancy.

It is with regret that we must now inform you that your present role with the Company is redundant. This decision is due to the Company (experiencing a downturn in work in recent months/having carried out a reorganisation of its business and activities for essential economic reasons).

At the meeting you were given the right to be accompanied and you chose to (waive this right/have in attendance. . . . .) *(insert name of work colleague or trade union official)*.

You are entitled to receive . . . . *(insert number)* (weeks/months) notice of the termination of your employment. You (are/are not) required to work out your notice period. We therefore confirm that your date of termination on the grounds of redundancy will be . . . . . *(insert date)*.

You will receive your P45 in due course and you will be paid the following:

* your normal salary up to the date of the termination of your employment
* a contractual redundancy payment of £ . . . . . *(insert amount)**
* a payment in lieu of your notice period since we do not require you to work out this period*
* a sum in respect of accrued but untaken annual leave entitlement*
* an ex gratia payment as compensation for loss of your employment of £. . . . . *(insert amount)**.

(*Delete as appropriate.)

Please note that in accordance with your contract of employment, the Company reserves the right to deduct from your final termination payment a sum in respect of any annual leave taken in excess of your accrued entitlement as at your termination date.

We would like to extend to you our best wishes for your future.

You have the right to appeal against the Company's decision if you are not satisfied with it. If you do wish to appeal, you must inform . . . . *(insert name of contact)* in writing within five working days of receiving this decision. If you do appeal, you will then be invited to attend an appeal meeting which you must take all reasonable steps to attend.

Yours sincerely,

. . . .
(Insert signature and name of author)

NOTIFICATION OF APPEAL MEETING

Date . . . . *(insert date)*

Dear . . . . *(insert name of employee)*

We refer to your letter dated . . . . . . *(insert date)* in which you lodged an appeal against your dismissal as confirmed to you in our letter dated . . . . . . *(insert date)*.

Your appeal against the Company's decision will be heard at an appeal meeting to take place on . . . . *(insert date)* at . . . . . . *(insert time)* at . . . . *(insert location)*. The appeal meeting will be chaired by . . . . *(insert name)*.

You have the right to be accompanied at the appeal meeting. Your companion may be either a work colleague or a trade union official of your choice. Your companion will be permitted to address the meeting and to confer with you during the meeting but they will not generally be permitted to answer any questions on your behalf. You should inform the chair of the appeal meeting in advance of the identity of your chosen companion.

If you or your chosen companion is unable to attend this appeal meeting, you are asked to contact . . . . *(insert contact name)* as a matter of urgency so that an alternative date and time can be scheduled. You should take all reasonable steps to attend the appeal meeting. Failure to attend without good reason could result in the meeting being held, and a decision being taken, in your absence. However, if you fail to attend through circumstances completely outside your control and which are currently unforeseeable, the Company will then arrange another appeal meeting. Thereafter, if you fail to attend for a second time, the meeting will be held, and a decision will be taken on your appeal, in your absence.

After the meeting, we will inform you in writing of the Company's decision. Please note that the decision made following this appeal meeting will be final and there will be no further right of appeal against it.

Yours sincerely,

. . . .

(Insert signature and name of author)

CONFIRMATION OF OUTCOME OF APPEAL MEETING

Date . . . . *(insert date)*

Dear . . . . *(insert name of employee)*

Further to the appeal meeting held on . . . . *(insert date)* relating to your dismissal as confirmed to you in our letter dated . . . . *(insert date)*, the Company has now taken a decision on your appeal, namely that the original dismissal decision (stands/is hereby revoked and your employment with the Company is therefore reinstated as if you had never been dismissed).

The reasons for this decision are as follows:

- *(List reasons for decision to uphold or revoke the original dismissal decision.)*

You have now exercised your right of appeal and this decision is final.

Appeal meeting conducted by: . . . . *(insert name)*

Yours sincerely,

. . . .
(Insert signature and name of author)

STATEMENT OF REASONS FOR DISMISSAL

Date. . . . . *(insert date)*

Dear . . . . *(insert name of employee)*

We refer to our letter dated . . . . *(insert date)* terminating your employment with the Company.

As you (are pregnant/on maternity leave/on adoption leave) you are entitled to receive a written statement of the reasons for your dismissal. We therefore confirm that the reasons for the termination of your employment are . . . . *(insert reasons)*.

OR

You have requested a written statement of the reasons for your dismissal. As you had at least one year's continuous employment with the Company, you are entitled to make that request. We are obliged to provide you with a written statement of the reasons for your dismissal within 14 days of receipt of your request. We received your request on . . . . *(insert date)*. We therefore confirm that the reasons for the termination of your employment were . . . . *(insert reasons)*.

Yours sincerely,

. . . .

(Insert signature and name of author)

EXIT QUESTIONNAIRE

It is both unfortunate and expensive when an employee decides to leave the Company. It is important that we find out the reason why so that we can try to avoid losing staff in the future. Once an employee has resigned, they are more likely to give an honest input, which is invaluable to the Company. We would therefore ask you to complete the following exit questionnaire and then return it to . . . . *(insert name of contact)*.

With your permission, selected information gained from this questionnaire will be discussed with your line manager. The aim of this is to ensure that any problem issues can be discussed and resolved before you leave. It also means that if we discover you are leaving as a direct result of perceived problems of which we were previously unaware, the Company can try to resolve these to the mutual satisfaction of all parties.

A copy of this questionnaire will also be placed on your personnel file.

Thank you for your comments.

Are you moving to start a new job?   YES / NO*
                                                      *(*delete as appropriate)*

What made you decide to leave the Company?

Is there anything the Company could have done to make you stay?

Have you been happy during your time with the Company?

Were you made to feel that your contribution was important?

What do you think you have you gained from your time with the Company?

Were you given sufficient opportunities for training and development? If not, what more did you need?

_____

What do you think is good about the Company?

_____

What could the Company improve on?

_____

Please add any other comments you wish to make. You may wish to comment on your place of work, the people you work with or the job that you do.

_____

Do you have any objection to this questionnaire being discussed with your line manager?

YES / NO*
(*Delete as appropriate.)

_____

Name: . . . . (insert name of employee)

Signed: . . . .

Date: . . . .

RESPONSE TO RESIGNATION

Date .... *(insert date)*

Dear .... *(insert name of employee)*

We refer to your resignation letter dated .... *(insert date)* and our meeting on .... *(insert date)* when we discussed your reasons for leaving. Whilst we are naturally disappointed with your decision to resign, we hereby confirm that we accept your resignation.

As you know, your contractual notice period is .... *(insert number)* (weeks/months). This means that your termination of employment date is .... *(insert date)*.

You will be paid your normal salary up to the date of the termination of your employment, together with a sum in respect of accrued but untaken annual leave entitlement (if any). If by your termination date you have taken more annual leave than you have accrued for the current holiday year, in accordance with your contract of employment, the Company reserves the right to deduct from your final termination payment a sum equivalent to the excess annual leave taken.

You will receive your P45 in due course.

We would like to extend to you our best wishes for your future and to thank you for all your efforts during your employment with the Company.

Yours sincerely,

....

(Insert signature and name of author)

EARLY RELEASE FROM NOTICE LETTER

Date . . . . *(insert date)*

Dear . . . . *(insert name of employee)*

We refer to your resignation letter dated . . . . *(insert date)* and our meeting on . . . . *(insert date)* when we accepted your resignation following discussions about your reasons for leaving.

As you know, your contractual notice period is . . . . *(insert number)* (weeks/months). This means that your termination of employment date was due to be . . . . *(insert date)*. However, at our meeting, you requested to leave early, on . . . . *(insert date)*.

We appreciate that you are keen to start your new job as soon as possible. Therefore, the Company has considered your request and hereby agrees to release you from your contractual obligation to serve out your notice period. As such, we confirm that your termination date will be brought forward to . . . . *(insert date)*. In return, you agree to release the Company from any further obligation to pay you after your revised termination date. Could you please complete the attached acceptance slip to confirm that you agree with these terms and then return it to . . . . *(insert name of contact)* by no later than . . . . *(insert date)*.

We would like to extend to you our best wishes for your future in your new job and to thank you for all your efforts during your employment with the Company.

Yours sincerely,

. . . .
(Insert signature and name of author)

Enc.

RESPONSE TO "HEAT OF THE MOMENT" RESIGNATION

Date . . . . *(insert date of letter)*

Dear . . . . *(insert name of employee)*

We refer to the events of earlier today, which culminated in your verbal resignation and your then leaving the Company's premises.

OR

We refer to your resignation letter dated . . . . *(insert date)* which we received today.

In view of the circumstances surrounding your departure and the comments made by you at that time, we are not willing at this stage to accept your resignation.

OR

In view of the serious issues raised by you in your resignation letter, we are not willing at this stage to accept your resignation.

Rather, we would like to invite you to attend a grievance meeting to discuss matters, with a view to reaching an amicable resolution enabling you to return to your job with the Company. In the circumstances, could I ask you to contact . . . . *(insert name of contact)* as a matter of urgency and, in any event, by no later than . . . . . . *(insert date)*. We will then arrange a grievance meeting with you to take place within the next couple of days at your convenience. At that meeting, we will be able to explore in detail recent events and the various issues raised.

You have the statutory right to be accompanied at the grievance meeting. Your companion may be either a work colleague or a trade union official of your choice. Your companion will be permitted to address the meeting and to confer with you during the meeting but they will not be permitted to answer questions on your behalf. You should inform the chair of the meeting in advance of the identity of your chosen companion.

You are required to take all reasonable steps to attend the grievance meeting once it has been arranged with you. Failure to attend without good reason could result in the meeting being held, and a decision being taken on your grievance, in your absence. However, if you fail to attend through circumstances completely outside your control and which are currently unforeseeable, the Company will arrange another meeting. Thereafter, if you fail to attend for a second time, the meeting will be held, and a decision on your grievance will be taken, in your absence.

After the grievance meeting, you will be informed in writing of the Company's decision.

However, if we do not hear from you by the date specified above, we will have no alternative but to reluctantly assume that you do not wish to have a grievance meeting and that instead you intend to stand by your resignation.

We look forward to hearing from you.

Yours sincerely,

. . . .

(Insert signature and name of author)

COMPROMISE AGREEMENT

THIS AGREEMENT is made on . . . . *(insert date)*

AND IS MADE BETWEEN:

. . . . Limited *(insert name of Company)* whose registered office is at . . . .
. . . . *(insert registered office details)* ("the Company"); and

. . . . *(insert name of employee)* of . . . . *(insert address of employee)*
("the Employee")

RECITALS:

1. The Employee has been employed by the Company under the terms of a contract of employment dated . . . . . . *(insert date)*.

2. This Agreement satisfies the conditions regulating compromise agreements under:

    * Section 203 of the Employment Rights Act 1996
    * Section 72 of the Race Relations Act 1976
    * Section 77 of the Sex Discrimination Act 1975
    * Section 9 of the Disability Discrimination Act 1995
    * Schedule 4 to the Employment Equality (Religion or Belief) Regulations 2003
    * Schedule 4 to the Employment Equality (Sexual Orientation) Regulations 2003
    * Regulation 35 of the Working Time Regulations 1998
    * Section 49 of the National Minimum Wage Act 1998
    * Section 288 of the Trade Union and Labour Relations (Consolidation) Act 1992.

3. The Employee has received independent legal advice from a solicitor, ...
(insert name of solicitor) of . . . . *(insert firm name)* of . . . . *(insert firm address)*, as to the terms and effect of this Agreement and, in particular, its effect upon their ability to pursue their rights in an employment tribunal. By signing this Agreement, ... *(insert firm name)* warrants that the solicitor who provided the advice holds a current practising certificate and that it currently maintains the level of indemnity cover required of it by the Law Society covering the risk of a claim by the Employee in respect of any loss arising in consequence of the advice they have received.

THE COMPANY AND THE EMPLOYEE AGREE AS FOLLOWS:

1. The employment of the Employee by the Company (will terminate/terminated) on . . . . *(insert date)* ("the Termination Date").

2. The Employee has notified the Company that they consider they are in a position to make a complaint of . . . . *(insert details of employee's complaint, for example unfair dismissal, sex discrimination, race discrimination, etc. and refer to any correspondence in which the employee has notified the Company of their complaint).*

3. The Company shall:

3.1. Pay the Employee their salary up to and including the Termination Date and pay in lieu of any accrued but unused annual leave entitlement. These sums will be subject to normal statutory income tax and national insurance deductions.

3.2. Without admission of any liability as claimed or otherwise, pay to the Employee by way of compensation for termination of employment the sum of £ . . . . *(insert amount)* within 14 days of the signing of this Agreement ('the Payment'). Of this sum, £ . . . . *(insert amount)* will be paid free of income tax and national insurance deductions and the balance of £ . . . . *(insert amount)* will be paid after the deduction of income tax and national insurance.

3.3. Provide the Employee with a P45 within 14 days of the signing of this Agreement.

3.4. Continue, up to and including . . . . . . *(insert date)*, to provide the Employee with the benefits of (*life assurance, private medical insurance and pension scheme contributions) on the same terms as those benefits were provided to the Employee as at the Termination Date.

3.5. Permit the Employee to retain their company car until . . . . *(insert date)* on the same terms and conditions as they enjoyed the use of that car during their employment but on the understanding that no mileage incurred by the Employee will constitute travel between their home and the Company's premises nor will it constitute business travel.

3.6. Provide the Employee with a reference in the attached terms should the same be requested by any potential employer of the Employee.

3.7. Contribute to the Employee's legal costs in seeking advice on this Agreement up to a maximum of £ . . . . *(insert amount)* plus VAT.

(*Delete as appropriate.)

4. The Employee shall:

4.1. Not divulge to any third party at any time any trade secrets or other confidential information belonging to the Company or any of its associated companies and not use such secrets or information for their own benefit or that of any third party.

4.2. Return to the Company all documents, software, keys, cards and any other property which belongs to the Company or relates in any way to the business of the Company or any associated company which are in their possession or under their control.

4.3. Refrain from disclosing the contents of the terms of this Agreement other than to their spouse, lawyer or accountant except as may be ordered by any court, government agency or as required by law.

4.4. Accept full responsibility for the payment of any income tax and national insurance deductions not already made by the Company and indemnify and keep indemnified the Company against all and any liabilities to tax or national insurance deductions which the Company may incur in respect of or by reason of the Payment.

4.5. Resign from their directorship with the Company with effect from the Termination Date, execute a letter of resignation in such form as the Company shall require and execute any further documents as may be necessary to give full effect to the resignation.

4.6. Accept the payments and actions of the Company set out above in full and final settlement of all or any claims arising out of their contract of employment or its termination which they may have against the Company or any associated company or any of its or their officers or employees. This provision applies whether such claims are contractual, statutory or otherwise and however they may arise. For the avoidance of doubt, such claims may include, but are not limited to, claims for breach of contract (whether brought before an employment tribunal or otherwise), redundancy pay, unfair dismissal, equal pay, discrimination or victimisation by reason of sex, race, disability, sexual orientation or religion or belief or unlawful deductions from wages. Further, the Employee waives any claim or right of action which the Employee may now have or which they may become aware of after the execution of this Agreement.

SIGNED:

. . . .

Director
For and on behalf of the Company

SIGNED:

. . . . *(insert name of employee)*

SIGNED:

. . . . *(insert name of solicitor)*
For and on behalf of . . . . *(insert name of firm)*

LETTER TO ACCOMPANY COMPROMISE AGREEMENT

Date . . . . *(insert date)*

Dear . . . . *(insert name of employee)*

WITHOUT PREJUDICE

We refer to our without prejudice meeting on . . . . *(insert date)* where we discussed the Company's proposal to terminate your employment with effect from . . . . *(insert date)*.

We enclose for your consideration a draft Compromise Agreement relating to the proposed termination of your employment. The draft sets out what we would propose to pay you as compensation for loss of your employment in return for your signing the Compromise Agreement.

You are required by law to take independent legal advice as to the terms and effect of the Compromise Agreement and, in particular, its effect on your ability to pursue your rights before an employment tribunal. You are able to take legal advice from:

A qualified lawyer (i.e. a barrister or a solicitor who holds a practising certificate), or

- an officer, official, employee or member of an independent trade union as long as that person has been certified in writing by the union as competent to give advice and authorised to do so on behalf of the union, or

- an advice centre worker who has been certified by the advice centre as competent to give advice and authorised to do so on behalf of the centre.

Once you have had the opportunity to take legal advice, we would request that your legal adviser contacts . . . . *(insert name of contact)* in order that the Compromise Agreement can be agreed and engrossments then produced for signature. Your legal adviser will need to be identified in and sign the Compromise Agreement.

We look forward to hearing from you. The terms set out in the Compromise Agreement will only be on offer until . . . . *(insert date)* and therefore we recommend you seek legal advice as a matter of urgency.

Yours sincerely,

. . . .
(Insert signature and name of author)

Enc.

Section X

Miscellaneous

ESSENTIAL
EMPLOYMENT
DOCUMENTS

Miscellaneous

In addition to the wide selection of precedent documents, policies, clauses and letters provided under the specific topic headings elsewhere in this book, we've concluded by bringing together a number of miscellaneous documents. These cover everything from probationary periods to appraisals.

PROBATIONARY PERIODS

When taking on new employees you might provide for a "probationary period". This is usually three to six months, although it could be longer or shorter. However, note that, in employment law terms, the labelling of an employee as a "probationer" has very little effect on the employer/employee relationship. Employees who have worked for you for less than a year do not have the general right to claim unfair dismissal, although there are a number of exceptions to this rule. Therefore, the reality is that employees who are placed on probation for less than a year will not be able to claim unfair dismissal if they are dismissed at the end of their probationary period.

Of course, the majority of probationary employees are entirely satisfactory and you will not want to dismiss them. In this case, use the ***Satisfactory Probationary Period Letter*** to confirm their continued employment. Alternatively, you might feel that an employee is not quite performing or behaving to the high standards you expect. Therefore, you would like to extend the probationary period to serve as a "warning" that an improvement in performance and/or conduct is needed if he wants to avoid being dismissed. In extending the probationary period, you will still need to comply with the statutory dismissal and disciplinary procedure. Use the ***Unsatisfactory Probationary Period Letter*** contained in the section on "Termination of Employment" followed by the ***Extension of Probationary Period Letter***.

258

UNAUTHORISED ABSENCE

It's not uncommon for employees to simply fail to report for work without providing any reason for their absence. This sometimes happens when an employee is due back from annual leave but where he's decided, of his own volition and without any approval, that he would like a few extra days off! More often, it happens without any warning or obvious explanation. In these circumstances, you need to be proactive. Your aim is to try and discover what has happened and whether or not the employee plans to return to work. The starting point is to telephone him. If that does not work, then you should write to the employee on his second day of absence asking him to make contact as a matter of urgency and giving him a reasonable deadline by which to do so, after which you will assume by his conduct that the employee has, in fact, resigned. The *Failure to Return from Holiday Letter* and the *Unauthorised Absence Letter* will help you here. With annual leave, ensure you have in place a formal system of approval for leave requests, so there can be no misunderstanding about exactly which days off have been granted as annual leave. The *Holiday Request Form* is a useful starting point for putting an appropriate system in place. Finally, bear in mind that unauthorised absence is a disciplinary matter, so if and when the employee does return to work, you can then deal with this in accordance with your disciplinary procedure. A formal warning may well be appropriate.

DATA PROTECTION

Under the **Data Protection Act 1998**, employees have the right, on written request, to access personal data that you hold about them which is stored either on computer (for example, in Word documents, databases or e-mails) or in a relevant paper-based filing system (for example, in individual personnel files or disciplinary records). You are able to charge the employee a fee of up to £10 for providing a copy of the personal data requested and you must comply with his (or an ex-employee's) request within 40 days. Confidential references, which you give for the purpose of training or employment, are excluded from this right. However, references given by third parties and received by you are not so excluded. If you have an employee who demands a copy of his personnel file, etc. then ask him to complete the *Personal Data Subject Access Request Form* first.

APPRAISALS

It's good performance management procedure to appraise your staff on a regular basis and, in any event, no less than once a year. A quarterly assessment together with a formal annual appraisal is a popular system for small to medium-sized employers. The aim of appraisals should not just be to explore performance and conduct during the relevant appraisal period but also to use this information to set targets and goals to be achieved during the forthcoming appraisal period. This will necessarily involve discussing future training needs and career development. In order to make the whole process worthwhile, the appraisal procedure should be a two-way discussion between you and your employee. The **Appraisal Procedure and Form** will assist you in implementing an appraisal system on which you can continue to build. Having a formal appraisal system in place is particularly important if you pay discretionary performance-related bonuses because, if challenged, you will need to be able to show that a decision on the payment or amount of a particular bonus was reasonable and not arbitrary. A detailed appraisal form will help you in justifying your decision.

APPRAISAL PROCEDURE AND FORM

Appraisal procedure

Each year in . . . . *(insert month)*, you will take part in an appraisal session with your line manager. The purpose of the meeting is to discuss your performance, conduct and achievements during the previous year and to define performance objectives and training and career development needs for the future.

The outcome of the meeting should be a clear action plan for both you and your line manager in order to enable you to achieve your full potential in your job and to gain maximum job satisfaction. In turn, this will contribute towards the Company's success.

Following the appraisal session, your line manager will complete an appraisal form as a record of the discussion that took place. This will also ensure that any agreed action points can be followed up with due diligence. You will then be asked to add your own comments to the form and to sign it to acknowledge that the various comments and action points contained therein have been discussed. If you are in substantial disagreement with the contents of the appraisal, you should record your viewpoint in the relevant section on the form.

Once the appraisal process has been completed, a copy of the completed appraisal form will be given to you for your own safekeeping and the original will be stored in confidence in your personnel file. The appraisal form (incorporating the action plan) must be viewed as a working document and should be continually referred to by both you and your line manager throughout the year.

If you feel that your appraisal was unfair you may make a request to . . . . *(insert name of contact)* for your appraisal to be reviewed. A more senior manager will conduct this review with both you and the relevant line manager.

Appraisal form for the year ending . . . . *(insert date)*

Name of employee:

Department and job title:

Date of appointment to current job:

Name of line manager completing the appraisal:

Date of next appraisal:

This form is used to record the discussion that takes place between you and your line manager on an annual basis. It covers a summary of the previous year's conduct and performance, both in terms of what has been achieved and how it has been achieved, and identifies what is required for the forthcoming year.

This form is in two parts. Part A should be completed by the line manager immediately after the appraisal session. Part B should then be completed by you. A copy of the completed form will be given to you and the original form will be placed on your personnel file.

The following performance levels are used in this form:

5 = Outstanding (consistently exceptional, performs far beyond the position requirements)

4 = Above expectations (usually performs beyond the position requirements)

3 = Meets expectations (consistently performs the position requirements)

2 = Needs improvement (improvement is needed to satisfy the position requirements)

1 = Unsatisfactory (falls far below the position requirements)

PART A – FOR COMPLETION BY THE LINE MANAGER

Please summarise the nature of the work undertaken by the employee.

Line manager's assessment of the employee's skills and knowledge.

Assessment of skills	5	4	3	2	1	N/A	Comments
Product knowledge							
Quality and accuracy of work							
Written communication skills							
Verbal Communication skills							
Work relationships							
Productivity and efficiency							
Achievement of targets							
Willingness to take on responsibility							
Ability to work without supervision							
Ability to perform under pressure							
Attendance record							
Timekeeping record							
Organisational skills							
Client satisfaction							

(insert additional skills)

List achievements during last year (include courses attended, specific targets achieved and significant projects undertaken).

. . . .

. . . .

. . . .

Line manager's views on the employee's overall performance and contribution to the Company in the previous year.

. . . .

. . . .

. . . .

Agreed targets and performance objectives for the forthcoming year (the action plan).

. . . .

. . . .

. . . .

Recommendations for training and career development in the coming year (including suggestions for alternative employment within the Company).

. . . .

. . . .

. . . .

Any further comments by the employee's line manager.

. . . .

. . . .

. . . .

PART B – FOR COMPLETION BY THE EMPLOYEE

Are there any other jobs that you would like to do within the Company?

. . . .

. . . .

. . . .

What are your work-related ambitions?. . . . .

. . . .

. . . .

. . . .

Please use this space to say how you felt about your appraisal session and any points you wish to make about the targets and performance objectives that have been agreed. If you disagree with your line manager's assessment of your performance and conduct, please record your comments here. . . . .

. . . .

. . . .

. . . .

Signed: . . . . Signed: . . . .
(insert name of line manager) *(insert name of employee)*

Date: . . . . Date: . . . .

EXTENSION OF PROBATIONARY PERIOD LETTER

Date .... *(insert date of letter)*

Dear .... *(insert name of employee)*

Further to the meeting held on ...... *(insert date)* regarding the Company's proposal to either dismiss you or to extend your probationary period, having reviewed your (performance/conduct), the Company has now decided that your probationary period will be extended by a further (one month/two months/three months) until ..... *(insert date)*, for the following reasons: .... *(list reasons for extension of probationary period)*.

At the meeting you were given the statutory right to be accompanied and you chose to (waive this right/have in attendance ......) *(insert name of work colleague or trade union official)*.

Naturally, we will continue to monitor your performance and conduct and we will formally review your progress at the end of the extended probationary period as well as providing you with our feedback on an ongoing basis. We must warn you that if you fail to make sufficient progress either during or by the end of your extended probationary period, this is likely to result in the termination of your employment. Please be aware that the Company may not be prepared to extend the probationary period again.

We hope that you will work with the Company to improve your (performance/conduct) so that termination of your employment will not be necessary. If there are any aspects of your performance or conduct you wish to discuss in the meantime, please speak to .... *(insert name of contact)*.

You have the right to appeal against the Company's decision if you are not satisfied with it. If you do wish to appeal, you must inform .... *(insert name of contact)* in writing within five working days of receiving this decision. If you do appeal, you will then be invited to attend an appeal meeting which you must take all reasonable steps to attend.

Yours sincerely,

....
(Insert signature and name of author)

FAILURE TO RETURN FROM HOLIDAY LETTER

Date . . . . *(insert date of letter)*

Dear . . . . *(insert name of employee)*

According to our Company records, you were due to attend for work on . . . . . . *(insert date)* following your period of annual leave. However, you have failed to report for work and we have not received any explanation from you for your non-attendance. On . . . . . . *(insert date)* at . . . . *(insert time)* . . . . *(insert name of contact)* did try to make contact with you by telephone (but there was no answer/but you were not available and so a message was left for you which you did not acknowledge).

Your conduct in failing to report for work without providing any reason whatsoever implies that you intend to, or have, resigned your position with the Company. If this is not your intention and you are proposing to return to work, we would ask you to contact . . . . *(insert name of contact)* as a matter of urgency and, in any event, by no later than . . . . *(insert time)* on . . . . *(insert date)*.

You will be asked to explain why you have both failed to report for work and to contact us and when you do expect to return to work. We must warn you that unauthorised absence without good reason is a serious disciplinary offence which could result in disciplinary action being taken against you in accordance with the Company's disciplinary procedure. Depending on the particular circumstances of the case, it may amount to gross misconduct.

However, if you have resigned, please supply us with a written resignation letter as soon as possible.

Yours sincerely,

. . . .
(Insert signature and name of author)

HOLIDAY REQUEST FORM

This form is to record requests for annual leave and is to be completed by the employee and countersigned by their line manager. It must be completed for all requests for annual leave of half a day or more.

Employees must not book holidays until their request for annual leave has been formally approved.

Full name of employee:

First working day of proposed annual leave:

Last working day of proposed annual leave:

Total number of working days of proposed annual leave:

Balance of annual leave entitlement remaining if this request is authorised:

Please give any information you would like your line manager to take into account in relation to this request:

I declare that the information I have given on this form is true and I understand that my request for annual leave is not authorised until my line manager has countersigned this form. I accept that any annual leave I purport to take without the prior authorisation of my line manager will be viewed by the Company as unauthorised absence, which is a serious disciplinary offence and could result in disciplinary action being taken against me in accordance with the Company's disciplinary procedure. I appreciate that it may amount to gross misconduct and therefore could result in my summary dismissal.

Signed: . . . .   Signed: . . . .
(insert name of employee)   *(insert name of manager)*

Date: . . . .   Date: . . . .

PERSONAL DATA SUBJECT ACCESS REQUEST FORM

You can use this form to make a request under the **Data Protection Act 1998** to receive a copy of personal data that the Company holds about you. Once completed, this form should be forwarded to .... *(insert name)*, the Company's Data Protection Officer, who will deal with your request.

Full name of applicant:
(Please provide any other names under which you have been employed)

_____

Are you an employee, ex-employee or job applicant?:

Employee/ex-employee/job applicant*
*(*Delete as appropriate)*

_____

Work location and employing department:

_____

Relevant employment dates (as applicable):

(a) Commencement date:

(b) Termination date:

(c) Date of job application:

(d) Date of job interview:

_____

Please specify precisely the personal data that you are requesting:

_____

Address to which you would like the personal data to be sent:

_____

Contact telephone number:

_____

By completing this form, I accept that I am making a request under the Data Protection Act 1998 to receive a copy of specified personal data that the Company holds about me. By signing below, I confirm that I am the data subject named above and that you may contact me to obtain further identifying information before agreeing to my request.

I enclose a cheque in the sum of £10.00 made payable to the Company. I understand that it may take up to 40 days from receipt of this form before a reply to my request is provided to me.

Signed: .... Date: ....

SATISFACTORY PROBATIONARY PERIOD LETTER

Date . . . . *(insert date)*

Dear . . . . *(insert name of employee)*

We refer to your offer of appointment letter dated . . . . *(insert date)* and your contract of employment dated . . . . *(insert date)*, both of which specified that your employment was subject to a (one/three/six) months' probationary period.

We have carefully monitored your performance and conduct during your probationary period, which ended on . . . . *(insert date)*. Now this period has come to an end, and having reviewed your performance and conduct, we are pleased to advise you that you have successfully completed your probationary period and we can therefore confirm your continued employment with the Company.

Naturally, we will continue to monitor your performance and conduct on an ongoing basis and we intend to provide a formal written assessment of your progress as part of the annual performance review programme in . . . . *(insert month)*. If there are any aspects of your performance or conduct, or indeed any other matters, you wish to discuss in the meantime, please speak to . . . . *(insert name of contact)*.

Yours sincerely,

. . . .
(Insert signature and name of author)

UNAUTHORISED ABSENCE LETTER

Date .... *(insert date of letter)*

Dear .... *(insert name of employee)*

According to our Company records, you failed to report for work on ...... *(insert date)* and you have not reported for work since that date. We have not received any explanation from you for your non-attendance. On ..... *(insert date)* at ..... *(insert time)* .... *(insert name of contact)* did try to make contact with you by telephone (but there was no answer/ but you were not available and so a message was left for you which you did not acknowledge).

Your conduct in failing to report for work without providing any reason whatsoever implies that you intend to, or have, resigned your position with the Company. If this is not your intention and you are proposing to return to work, we would ask you to contact .... *(insert name of contact)* as a matter of urgency and, in any event, by no later than ...... *(insert time)* on .... *(insert date)*.

You will be asked to explain why you have both failed to report for work and to contact us and when you do expect to return to work. We must warn you that unauthorised absence without good reason is a serious disciplinary offence which could result in disciplinary action being taken against you in accordance with the Company's disciplinary procedure. Depending on the particular circumstances of the case, it may amount to gross misconduct.

However, if you have resigned, please supply us with a written resignation letter as soon as possible.

Yours sincerely,

....

(Insert signature and name of author)